Following
WHO AM I?
HUMAN IDENTITY AND THE GOSPEL IN A CONFUSING WORLD
GW00642563
"A Fantastically helpful book"
ANDY BANNISTER
THOMAS FRETWELL
DayOne

First printed 2019
ISBN 978-1-84625-644-8

A CIP record is held at the British Library

Published by Day One Publications, Ryelands Road, Leominster, HR6 8NZ
☎ 01568 613 740
FAX 01568 611 473

email—sales@dayone.co.uk
web site—www.dayone.co.uk

Cover design by Sarah Fretwell
Printed by TJ International

To my Dad,
an example of sacrificial love.
'As a father . . . so the LORD' (Psalm 103:13).

I have read many books by many good authors on subjects similar to those in Tommy Fretwell's book Who Am I? *and I believe that this book ranks right up there with the best of them. This book is excellent for those who believe. But it is also relevant for those who have yet to believe that there is a God who made them, loves them and has a wonderful plan for their lives. I highly recommend it!*

Brian Brodersen, Pastor, Calvary Chapel, Costa Mesa, CA, USA

This book explores fundamental questions about human existence, identity, purpose and a relationship with God. Despite drawing on a strong scholarly background (the author holds two degrees in theology and is currently engaged in doctoral research), Thomas Fretwell offers a highly accessible and clear treatment of key theological, apologetic, philosophical and cultural issues. As such, this book is a must-read for everyday Christians seeking to understand, live and share their faith in today's rapidly changing culture. It will also be of considerable interest to non-Christians grappling with some of the questions it explores.

Dr Calvin Smith, Principal of King's Evangelical Divinity School, UK

Discovering the true nature, meaning and purpose of life has been mankind's desire since the dawn of antiquity. Many have attempted an answer, whether theists or non-theists. Who am I? *tackles this vital subject in a uniquely refreshing fashion. The author is adept in his treatment of matters historical, philosophical, sociological and theological, even weaving in some of his own compelling fictional writing along the way. Well documented but contemporary in its feel, this book takes the reader on a rich journey of exploration into the nature of human identity, inexorably leading to the full-orbed realization that the answers reside in a Person—the One who epitomized a fulfilled life and is its ultimate Source.*

Philip Bell, CEO, CMI-UK/Europe

A great man once said that the two most important studies are what a person is and what God is. He then stated that you can know what a person is only by knowing what God is. In this book, with biblical wisdom, with intelligent readings of our culture and with brilliantly chosen examples of its arguments, Thomas Fretwell shows the enduring wisdom of this observation. The question of identity is still our starting question. Who are we? Why? Want to know? Yes, you do: you're a person. To find yourself, you must know the One who put you here. You'd do very well to start here.

Ben Virgo, Director, Christian Heritage, London

What is a human being? Are we just random collocations of atoms, nothing more than a pack of neurons, or genetic puppets dancing to our DNA? Unless we properly know what (or who) we are we can't begin to tackle the bigger questions of life's meaning and purpose. Tommy Fretwell tackles these questions head-on in this fantastically helpful book, and whether you're a sceptic or a seeker, a doubter or a disciple, he'll help you see why the good news of Jesus offers the securest foundation for that most important of questions: what does it mean to be human?

Andy Bannister, apologist and director of the Solas Centre for Public Christianity, Dundee, UK

Acknowledgements

There are a number of people who have helped me in this project whom I would like to thank. Firstly, my wife Sarah. You have always been my shining light, an example of a faithful wife and mother. Thank you for picking up the slack whenever I disappeared into my study. Also, I thank my two boys, Jacob and Tobias, for the joy you bring into my life. And I thank my parents for their endless support in all things, and the rest of my family for their encouragement.

Thank you to those who kindly read and suggested improvements to the manuscript in its early stages. A special thank you to those who supported this project and provided me with teaching opportunities. I am very grateful to those who wrote endorsements for the book: Brian Brodersen, Philip Bell, Andy Bannister, Calvin Smith and Ben Virgo. Also, I am grateful to the team at Day One for taking on the book.

I would also like to thank my pastor, Doug Keen, for his input into my life. He is a faithful shepherd and co-labourer in the Lord. And I thank all my church family for their prayers and support.

Finally, I would like to mention Talia Butchers, a fellow Bible geek, whose many thoughtful questions and theological discussions helped shape much of the material in this book.

Contents

1 Introduction

Who am I? Just three words—six letters—make up this question. Yet the attempts to find a satisfying answer have produced enough words to fill countless libraries. To answer the question of who we are, we also need to ask: What we are? What does it mean to be human? Do we have a grand purpose, an end game towards which our lives are heading? Will anything we do have any real, lasting significance, or do we simply live a certain number of days on this planet before we cease to exist? During this time must we seek to carve out some sort of meaning for ourselves? If we live another forty years, that is only about 14,500 days. Start counting!

The implications of these questions are so far-reaching that they demand our attention. All over the globe today top universities are holding conferences and seeking answers from the brightest minds about what it means to be human. Experts from many disciplines have attempted to answer this question. Yet why is it that no consistent answer can be found? It seems odd that humans have been on this planet for so long, yet we still cannot answer even this fundamental question.

Who am I? Now before you simply dismiss this question as some abstract philosophical concept or see it as a question reserved for edgy teenagers, we must admit that problems of identity surface at all ages and in many different circumstances. In fact, answering these questions has an immensely practical side. This becomes clear in the way we navigate the daily decisions we have to make, as well as respond to the issues thrust upon us by our culture.

The way we approach our personal relationships, sexual ethics, issues of human rights, justice, and ultimately how we decide between right and wrong are intricately tied up in the concept of what it means to be human. These broad categories will play out in our lives in routine ways. For example, should I forgive that person who wronged me? Should I support this war? What political party should I support? Am I all alone? What should I watch on Netflix?

IS THERE MEANING TO LIFE?

All these issues, one way or another, relate back to three foundational principles: meaning, value and purpose. Do we as human beings have any ultimate meaning to our lives? Do we have any intrinsic worth? And for what purpose are we living? For centuries debate has raged in our culture around these issues. Perhaps the sharpest divide has been between those who accept the existence of God and those who reject God.

As polarized as these two sides may be, there is no denying that these questions are being raised by many different people, whether religious or not. The Internet search engine Ask Jeeves compiled a list of what it called the top 10 'unanswerable' questions of the past decade. The list was based on some 1.1 billion queries made on the site. Fascinatingly, the question ranked at number one was, 'What is the meaning of life?', with question number two being, 'Is there a God?' People are searching for meaning and it seems we have a natural propensity to seek this meaning in some transcendent cause outside of ourselves. Most people understand that the reality of God would provide meaning to their lives. The connection people have made is accurate. From a Christian perspective, it is easy to see how life is given objective meaning, value and purpose by the existence of God. Perhaps the simplest summary is found in the Westminster Shorter Catechism, which asks, 'What is the chief end of man?' and answers, 'Man's chief end is to glorify God and enjoy him for ever.' In addition, as beings created in the image of God, for the purpose of communing with God, our lives are endowed with inherent dignity and value.

Of course, without God there is no transcendent being to endow our lives with any ultimate meaning or purpose, a fact that has not gone unrecognized by many of the world's leading atheists. Consider the words of Bertrand Russell, one of the best-known atheists of the past generation:

> That Man is the product of causes which had no prevision of the end they were achieving; that his origin, his growth, his hopes and fears, his loves and his beliefs, are but the outcome of accidental collocations of atoms; that no fire, no heroism, no intensity of thought and feeling, can preserve an individual life beyond the grave; that all the labours of the ages, all the devotion, all the inspiration, all the noonday brightness of human genius, are destined to extinction in the vast death of the solar system, and that the whole temple of Man's achievement must inevitably be buried beneath the debris of a universe in ruins—all these things, if not quite beyond dispute, are yet so nearly certain, that no philosophy which rejects them can hope to stand. Only within the scaffolding of these truths, only on the firm foundation of unyielding despair can the soul's habitation be safely built.[1]

A more contemporary voice with the same message is atheist Alex Rosenberg. In his book *The Atheist's Guide to Reality* he says, 'What is the purpose of the universe? There is none. What is the meaning of life? Ditto . . . Does history have any meaning or purpose? It's full of sound and fury, signifying nothing.'[2]

Truly the future looks bleak from this vantage point! Despite recognizing that this worldview is unliveable, many atheists will still try to deny the logical conclusion that a universe without God is meaningless. Here they encounter a problem: in atheism the universe is a closed system; it is like a box with the lid firmly closed. They cannot appeal to some transcendent cause outside the box for meaning, so they must find meaning within. As the film director Stanley Kubrick once put it, 'The very meaninglessness of life forces man to create his own meaning. However vast the darkness, we must supply our own light.'[3] The late atheist Christopher Hitchens described how he responded to Christians who quizzed him about how he found meaning in life: 'A life that partakes even a little of friendship, love, irony, humour, parenthood, literature, and music, and the chance to take part in battles for the liberation of others cannot be called "meaningless".'[4]

An immediate question arises from this: what of lives that never have these things? Can they then be called meaningless? These categories are totally arbitrary and subjective. What is to stop someone else providing a different list of things that supposedly give their life meaning? What if their list contained something objectionable to you—say, the eradication of a particular people group? Suddenly the 'meaning of life' has taken a turn for the worse! But the only way to differentiate between their list and your list would be to smuggle in some objective values from outside the box. Nobel Prize-winning physicist and atheist Steven Weinberg concludes his book *The First Three Minutes* by stating that human life is 'a more-or-less farcical outcome of a chain of accidents reaching back to the first three minutes' and that the universe is doomed to face a 'future extinction of endless cold or intolerable heat'. Yet still he tries to find a silver lining in what this means for mankind, saying, 'The effort to understand the universe is one of the very few things that lifts human life a little above the level of farce, and gives it some of the grace of tragedy.'[5]

Given that he is an atheist physicist, it should come as no surprise that he extols the scientific endeavour as that which can provide life with a small measure of fulfilment and meaning, but what of the average person who works a regular nine-to-five job and may not believe in God? How can they lift their existence above the level of farce? Weinberg is quite right in describing this view of humanity as a 'tragedy'. It is no wonder that many of the early French existentialist philosophers such as Albert Camus reasoned that if God does not exist, life is absurd—and, more than that, positively cruel. In light of this, Camus reasoned, the only real philosophical answer is suicide. Tragically, many who have struggled with these issues, particularly among the younger generation, have seen this as a very real option.

WHAT DIFFERENCE DOES IT MAKE?

So who cares? Why does it matter what makes us human, and how does that concern us now as we struggle to understand ourselves amongst the joys and pains of life? It matters because what is true of us collectively impacts us individually. The understanding of who we are as humans—whether a random collection of atoms or a uniquely designed creature—forms the foundation of our identity. The question of how God relates to the issue of identity is pivotal and is something we cannot get away from, no matter how hard we try. In the book of Ecclesiastes, Solomon wrote these words: 'He has made everything beautiful in its time. Also, he has put eternity into man's heart, yet so that he cannot find out what God has done from the beginning to the end' (Ecclesiastes 3:11). We were made with eternity in our hearts—that is, we are specifically intended to find our ultimate meaning and fulfilment by living in accord with what we have been designed for: to glorify God and enjoy Him for ever. Either we deny God but still end up smuggling in certain objective categories that come from God, or we take the claims of Christ seriously: we investigate what it is He says about human nature, and we discover that the truth about who we are, or what we can be in Him, is even more glorious than we could ever have imagined.

Finding our true identity is tied up with answering the question which Jesus first asked his disciple Peter: 'Who do you say that I am?' (Matthew 16:15). Matthew's Gospel records that Peter replied, 'You are the Christ, the Son of the living God.' It was upon this expression of Peter's faith that Jesus said He would build the church. The foundation of the church is a recognition of the true identity of Jesus.

This question is crucial. If you have answered it in a similar way to Peter, with an expression of trust and acceptance of who Christ is and what He has done for you, then your position and your identity are, like Peter's, totally entwined with Christ. This identity is more beautiful than any self-conceived image or any identity fashioned in this world could ever be. In this book we will explore the question of human identity and look at what the 'riches of [God's] grace, which he lavished upon us' (Ephesians 1:7–8) truly are. This will involve examining some life-changing truths, along with confronting some of the more uncomfortable facts about ourselves.

My hope is that, in the end, you will be able to see that the identity Jesus offers is the only one that matters. More than that, compared with what the world can offer, compared with any identity cobbled together from items solely 'inside the box', the identity available through a relationship with Christ far surpasses them all. This identity relates to every area of your life. It weaves together your past, your present and your future in a way that only an all-knowing God can do, infusing every moment, the good and the bad, with everlasting significance.

Perhaps you have never considered how you might answer Jesus' question; it had never occurred to you that this question is even related to discovering who you are. Maybe you are simply struggling amidst turbulent situations in your life, seeking acceptance and belonging or going through pain or grief, and wondering 'Why?' Any number of circumstances in life can cause us to search for meaning and a true understanding of who we are. If this is you, I believe there is only one solution that can provide a satisfactory answer to these questions: Jesus. You see, if Christ is who He claims to be, and God exists, it changes everything. He exists eternally 'outside the box', yet in the person of Christ He voluntarily entered 'the box' in order to rescue us from our predicament and to tell us the truth about who we are and what our purpose in existing right now really is. Jesus Himself highlighted this point when He said, 'For this purpose I was born and for this purpose I have come into the world—*to bear witness to the truth*. Everyone who is of the truth listens to my voice' (John 18:37).[6]

The truth is that God made this world to be inhabited by us (Isaiah 45:18), and He created man for His glory (Isaiah 43:6–7) and to enjoy Him for ever (Psalm 16:11). He is the Author of life (Acts 3:15) and therefore the only one who can give us a truthful description of who we are (Romans 3:23). He knows us intimately (Matthew 10:30), cares for us immeasurably (1 Peter 5:7), loves us unconditionally (Romans 5:8) and offers us an abundant life (John 10:10). Such a life can only be realized by living in relationship with the one who made us—through correctly answering the question 'Who do you say that I am?'

That is the *truth*!

NOTES OVERLEAF ➡

Notes

1 Bertrand Russell, *Mysticism and Logic: Including a Free Man's Worship* (London: Unwin Paperbacks, 1986), pp. 10–11.

2 Alex Rosenberg, *The Atheist's Guide to Reality: Enjoying Life without Illusions* (New York: W. W. Norton, 2011), p. 3.

3 Quoted in Maria Popova, 'Stanley Kubrick on Mortality, the Fear of Flying, and the Purpose of Existence: 1968 Playboy Interview', BrainPickings, https://www.brainpickings.org/2012/07/26/stanley-kubrick-playboy-interview/.

4 Christopher Hitchens, *Hitch-22: A Memoir* (London: Atlantic, 2011), p. 331.

5 Steven Weinberg, *The First Three Minutes* (London: Andre Deutsch, 1977), pp. 154–155.

6 All emphasis in Scripture quotes throughout the book has been added.

2 Who am I?

The novel *Les Misérables* by Victor Hugo is considered one of the greatest literary works of the nineteenth century. It has been adapted for both stage and screen multiple times, becoming the longest-running musical ever. You may have seen the musical or watched the 2012 screen adaptation starring Hugh Jackman and Russell Crowe. The story touches on some fascinating subjects as it examines the intersection of law and grace through the lives of the convict Jean Valjean (Jackman) and police inspector Javert (Crowe). Jean Valjean is an ex-convict who escaped his punishment and is being relentlessly pursued across France by Javert, who is intent on bringing him to justice. Along the way Jean Valjean is shown mercy by a bishop who encourages him to turn his life around. Years later he takes these words to heart and under an alias, Monsieur Madeleine, he becomes a changed man. Rising to prominence in the city, he becomes known for his charitable works, is elected mayor of the city and rejuvenates its economy, creating many jobs for the people.

During one climactic scene Jean Valjean, under his alias, is confronted by Inspector Javert, who informs him that they have in custody a man Javert believes is the convict Valjean. Rather than allow an innocent man to be punished in his place, Valjean turns himself in to Javert. The intense struggle within Valjean as he prepares to make known his true identity to Javert is captured in the song 'Who Am I?'

Who am I?
Can I conceal myself for evermore?
Pretend I'm not the man I was before? . . .

Who am I? Who am I?
I'm Jean Valjean!

IDENTITY CRISIS

Jean Valjean was tormented by his past, always afraid that someone would find out his real identity and expose his life as a lie. We live in an era of secret identities. Popular superhero characters such as Batman, Superman and Spiderman all draw us into a world of fantasy where we can escape from reality and assume an alter ego. How often do we talk about Bruce Wayne, Clark Kent or Peter Parker? It is the fantasy identity we desire. The imagination is an amazing thing, but there is a danger that comes with it. With the advent of social media, it is all too easy to experiment with different identities. On-screen, we may present to people a completely different image from the person we really are. A few people might wonder what their 'true' sexual orientation is and experiment with an alternative identity for a period of time. Others might wish to experience a jet-setting lifestyle that will be the envy of their friends. Such is our consumerist age where we imagine there is a plethora of acceptable 'identities' available to us and we can simply pick and choose the one we like, or at least present to others the one we feel we should have.

This was graphically illustrated for me on a train journey to London. It was early afternoon and two girls were sitting opposite me and my family. They were dressed up ready for a night out, and there were a number of empty cans of alcoholic drink on the table between them. The girls' solemn faces stared vacantly out the window watching the world pass by; for at least thirty minutes not a word was spoken between them and not a pleasantry exchanged—not even a smile. Then, all of a sudden, I noticed one of the girls get out her phone, rearrange the empty cans on the table to fit the shot, take a photo and caption it, perhaps along the lines of 'Friday night is going to be insane'. She then uploaded it to Snapchat. She wanted her friends to see this: they would assume that she was engaged in another wild night out. But the reality was much bleaker; in fact, I have rarely seen two girls looking more miserable.

A particular image was being presented—but it wasn't real. The image revolved around an activity—in this case, showing people how much fun they were having. Too often we allow other people's perceptions to become the basis for our identity. It is easy to fall into this trap; we often identify with the things we do. When we meet someone we first ask their name, then, 'What do you do?' They might reply, 'I'm a doctor', 'I work for this charity' or 'I'm a student'; often it is easy to hang our identity on our vocation or our social group. But these things are temporal and uncertain, changing many times throughout our lives.

For others, their identity is defined by past negative events in their lives, maybe a history of substance abuse or a broken marriage. Still others find their identity solely on the basis of community or sexual orientation. These things are not unimportant, but they are not able to provide an objective identity. Additionally, to limit a person's entire identity to such things is to devalue the fullness of human identity. Yet for many, seeing no alternative, and with the frightening prospect of meandering through life without a coherent identity, they cobble one together from whatever they can. They cling to these things as if their very lives depended on it. But without any transcendent source of meaning or purpose they cannot really have a final destination in mind; they are just drifting through the sea of life hoping to find something that authenticates their identity in this world.

We all go through identity crises at different stages of our lives. Teenagers experience that search for self-expression as they slowly become independent from their parents and encounter different views about the world. Adults also go through periods of re-evaluation and doubt as to their identity. Perhaps our lives haven't taken the path we wanted or expected, we never achieved what we thought we would, or we are unable to determine the right direction for our lives. These things can leave a strong feeling of disillusionment and frustration, causing us to ponder questions of existence and purpose as we seek to find fulfilment in life.

A NOBLE QUESTION

If you are asking these questions, you are not alone; actually, you are in very good company. The search for identity and for the meaning of human existence is a theme that has occupied the minds of human beings for millennia. It has filled the pages of our works of art and drama, our songs and poems. As King Lear cried out in Shakespeare's play, 'Does anyone here know who I am? . . . Who can tell me who I am?'[1]

Holy men, sages, gurus, philosophers and scientists have

attempted to answer the perplexing question of man's existence. Often the answers have achieved nothing more than to highlight the great gaps that exist in man's understanding. Are we all rational, free-willed, conscious individuals? Or are we simply the physical outcome of a wholly physical process, with all concepts of self and consciousness being nothing more than an illusion created by chemical processes in the brain?

The latter view was very clearly presented in an interview between Oxford scholar and author of *The God Delusion* Richard Dawkins and comedian Ricky Gervais:

DAWKINS: It is amazing that this conscious being, this thinking being that is me, and that thinking being that is you, is actually produced by millions of nerve impulses whizzing around inside our brain. I mean, that is a magical thought.

GERVAIS: It is great, isn't it—we are in each other's dream. Even if free will is an illusion, it makes no difference. It makes a difference to us.

DAWKINS: I feel as though I have free will, even if I don't.

GERVAIS: Of course. And, you know, I'd say determinism is sound. But it is when they start making these leaps that we can't be responsible for our own actions. Well, you've still got to lock someone up if they go around murdering people to protect the innocent.

DAWKINS: Yes. It wasn't me that did the murder . . . it was my neurons and my genes.

GERVAIS: Of course, . . . it doesn't work. There is obviously a little bit of that creeping into everything—responsibility, being adult about things. But . . . it doesn't change a thing. I feel that I make my own choices, and if I don't, I certainly feel like I am choosing. So . . . it is not even worth worrying about. But . . . this thing that takes the art out of something or the humanity or the beauty—why? Why does it? It is strange.[2]

The transcript is illuminating in many ways. It illustrates that a materialist has no place for non-physical entities such as free will and independent minds, yet it also shows how hard it is to completely expunge these concepts from real life. Their solution is simply to state that it's OK because as long as they feel that they make their own choices, it doesn't matter! This is a problem: surely if you believe a thing to be true when it is actually false, then you are the one who is deluded? If you do not actually have free will, even if you think you do, then there is no significance morally or otherwise to anything you do. They are, however, both happy to live under this delusion. In Dawkins' case, isn't it very odd for someone who has made a career out of denigrating the 'irrational', deluded belief of Christians?

Ironically, this type of attitude is what the French atheist Jean-Paul Sartre called 'bad faith', a way of describing people who choose to live dishonestly by adopting false values in order to do away with the burden of freedom and all that it entails. Or, to bring this even more up to date, it is a choice between the red pill and the blue pill. In the film *The Matrix* the main character Neo (Keanu Reeves) discovers that the matrix is an illusory digital world created to prevent humans from discovering that they are being kept as slaves by a race of sentient machines. In the film, Morpheus, a messiah-type character, holds out his hand and offers Neo two pills. He then says,

> This is your last chance. After this, there is no turning back. You take the blue pill—the story ends, you wake up in your bed and believe whatever you want to believe. You take the red pill—you stay in Wonderland, and I show you how deep the rabbit hole goes. Remember: all I'm offering is the truth. Nothing more.

The blue pill will allow him to continue living under the delusion of reality that the matrix offers him; the red pill means he will see the painful truth of reality for what it is. It seems that for hardened materialists like Dawkins and Gervais, they are content with taking the blue pill and living under the delusion their worldview forces them to hold: that they have no freedom, even though the reality of freedom is a daily experience.

LESSONS FROM SPACE

Many of us do not really try to analyse the problem on such a philosophical level. It is quite possible to simply entertain the almost intuitive notion that 'there must be more than this'. In the Bible there is a book called Psalms. It is a wonderful collection of poetical writings that teach us many things about human nature and the character of God. In Psalm 8 the renowned king of Israel, David, is musing about existence as he gazes into the night sky. He then asks a question about humanity:

> When I look at your heavens, the work of your fingers,
> the moon and the stars, which you have set in place,
> what is man that you are mindful of him,
> and the son of man that you care for him?
>
> (Psalm 8:3–4)

In a later psalm he asks a similar question:

O LORD, what is man that you regard him,
  or the son of man that you think of him?
Man is like a breath;
  his days are like a passing shadow.

(Psalm 144:3–4)

David looks at the heavens and the vastness of the universe and ponders what God must be like to have created such a place. He sees the frailty of humanity in comparison to the eternal God and asks, why would one so great concern himself with man?

You may have had similar thoughts. Staring up into the starry heavens on a clear night can be an awe-inspiring experience. Seeing the beauty of a sunset can cause us to start using terms like 'work of art' or 'masterpiece'. Those with no particular religious outlook will often resort to complimenting 'mother nature'. Usually a work of art requires an artist who is deserving of praise, so personifying 'nature' seems to provide a way for people to talk about the beauty of the world while avoiding the conclusion that there must be a cause behind such beauty. Although many deny it, it is actually quite logical to make this connection and have these feelings. Christians call this 'natural revelation' as the Bible shows that the purpose of nature is to make us contemplate the existence of God.

In Psalm 19:1–4 we read these words:

The heavens declare the glory of God,
  and the sky above proclaims his handiwork.
Day to day pours out speech,
  and night to night reveals knowledge.
There is no speech, nor are there words,

whose voice is not heard.
Their voice goes out through all the earth,
and their words to the end of the world.

In the New Testament we find this same teaching powerfully expressed in Romans 1:19–20: 'For what can be known about God is plain to [mankind], because God has shown it to them. For his invisible attributes, namely, his eternal power and divine nature, have been clearly perceived, ever since the creation of the world, in the things that have been made. So they are without excuse.'

How can man not seek answers to his existence when confronted by the power and majesty so clearly visible in creation? This is driven home by what occurred in 1968 with the crew of *Apollo 8* on the first manned mission to leave the earth's orbit. Unique to this mission was the crew's opportunity to become the first people to see the dark side of the moon and witness the earth rise from behind it. This was an amazing accomplishment and testimony to man's ability, but there was another event that occurred on the *Apollo 8* mission. As the spacecraft orbited the moon, the crew became the first people to lay eyes upon a view of earth that, until this point, had been reserved for God alone. When they saw the globe appear to rise over the horizon of the moon, that beautiful blue marble suspended upon the black canvas of space, what did they do? What words could be found to describe this awe-inspiring moment? Was it a declaration that the things they were seeing amounted to nothing but the fortunate product of random chance? Was it the words of Russell, that we are just an 'accidental collocation of atoms'? Was it an announcement that the universe is meaningless? No! The only words that were suited to such a moment were the words from the book of Genesis: 'In the beginning God created the heavens and the earth.'

As *Apollo 8* orbited the earth the astronauts read from the book of Genesis. The flight transcript is available in the NASA archives. The three crew members, Frank Borman, Jim Lovell and Bill Anders, took it in turns to read:

ANDERS: We are now approaching lunar sunrise, and for all the people back on Earth, the crew of Apollo 8 has a message that we would like to send to you.

. . . In the beginning God created the Heaven and the Earth. And the Earth was without form, and void; and darkness was upon the face of the deep. And the spirit of God moved upon the face of the waters, and God said, 'Let there be light.' And there was light. And God saw the light, that it was good, and God divided the light from the darkness . . .

LOVELL: And God called the light Day, and the darkness he called Night. And the evening and the morning were the first day. And God said, 'Let there be a firmament in the midst of the waters, and let it divide the waters from the waters.' And God made the firmament and divided the waters which were under the firmament from the waters which were above the firmament. And it was so. And God called the firmament Heaven. And the evening and the morning were the second day . . .

BORMAN: And God said, 'Let the waters under the Heavens be gathered together unto one place. And let the dry land appear.' And it was so. And God called the dry land Earth. And the gathering together of the waters called he seas. And God saw that it was good. And from the crew of Apollo 8, we close with good night, good luck, a Merry Christmas and God bless all of you— all of you on the good Earth.[3]

This message was broadcast live across the globe. In a touch of providential irony, the broadcast was aired on 24 December 1968. As millions across the planet were preparing to celebrate the birth of Christ in a manger, God was reminding them that the one they celebrated as a helpless babe was also the one who had created this vast universe!

TWO RESPONSES, TWO PATHS

For many, the reverence of the situation seemed appropriate: to attribute the beauty of the cosmos to the power of a creator God was the only sensible response. Yet for some, that was unacceptable. The founder of American Atheists, Madalyn Murray O'Hair, responded by attempting to sue the United States Government for breach of First Amendments rights. Thankfully, she did not get far. Yet many share her disdain for the idea of attributing the universe to the work of a creator. For those who reject a biblical universe, either through the acceptance of naturalistic philosophies or simply by default due to never having actually thought about it, the vastness of the universe is frequently hailed as that which demonstrates the insignificance of man and refutes the theistic notion that humans have some privileged position in the universe. Listen to the words of the astronomer Carl Sagan, who became famous for his hit 1980's US TV series *Cosmos: A Personal Voyage*:

Look again at that dot. That's here. That's home. That's us. On it everyone you love, everyone you know, everyone you ever heard of, every human being who ever was, lived out their lives. The aggregate of our joy and suffering, thousands of confident religions, ideologies, and economic doctrines, every hunter and forager, every hero and coward, every creator and destroyer of civilization, every king and peasant, every young couple in love, every mother and father, hopeful child, inventor and explorer, every teacher of morals, every corrupt politician, every 'superstar', every 'supreme leader', every saint and sinner in the history of our species lived there—on a mote of dust suspended in a sunbeam . . . Our posturing, our imagined self-importance, the delusion that we have some privileged position in the Universe, are challenged by this point of pale light. Our planet is a lonely speck in the great enveloping cosmic dark. In our obscurity, in all this vastness, there is no hint that help will come from elsewhere to save us from ourselves.[4]

It is easy to sense the almost religious overtures to this paragraph as it specifically seeks to counter the Christian concept of man. Yet for all the scientific posturing about empirical data, this viewpoint about the universe is more of a philosophical position than a scientific one, as the tag line to the TV show proves: every episode of the TV series began with this classic phrase from Sagan, 'The Cosmos is all that is, or ever was, or ever will be.' This trademark slogan makes it wonderfully clear that Sagan's naturalistic philosophy is being offered as an explicit substitute for Christianity, for the slogan itself is supposed to be a substitute for the famous Christian confession known as the Gloria Patri:

Glory be to the Father, and to the Son:
and to the Holy Ghost;
As it was in the beginning, is now, and ever shall be:
world without end. Amen.[5]

It is easy to see that if this is true, Sagan's slogan is not;

but if Sagan's philosophy is true and the material universe is all there has ever been or will be, then there is no room for the supernatural, and thus no God. In this naturalistic framework the universe itself takes on a divine quality as the eternal uncaused cause. Sagan was explicit in pushing his naturalistic God-substitute as he often said that humans are but 'children of the cosmos', and he even went so far as to say that 'Our ancestors worshiped the Sun, and they were far from foolish', for if we must worship something, 'does it not make sense to revere the sun and the stars?'[6] That is quite an amazing statement. However, for those followers of the naturalistic prophets who imagine this to be a conclusion based upon scientific investigation, it is not; it is based on a prior commitment to philosophical naturalism, which at its heart is a rejection of God. I quoted earlier from Romans 1:19–20, which explains how God's eternal power and divine attributes can be clearly seen through creation; but that passage then goes on to explain why people reject God: 'because they exchanged the truth about God for a lie and worshipped and served the creature rather than the Creator, who is blessed for ever! Amen' (Romans 1:25). There you have it: they worshipped the created things rather than the Creator! Written around two thousand years ago, it describes perfectly the actions of Sagan and his followers who have rejected God and replaced Him with the cosmos itself.

THE OTHER OPTION

This is one way to respond, but not the only way. For why must the impressive, incalculable size of the universe necessarily lead to the conclusion that we are insignificant? This is not what King David meant when he looked at the heavens and asked, 'What is man that you regard him?' He was expressing quite the opposite thought: how amazing it is that a God with the power to create the heavens has chosen to make mankind the centrepiece of his creation! Why does God so clearly love man and seek to save him? So why is the vastness of the universe used to argue that God does not exist?

It is sometimes said that if this tiny planet is the focus of the entire universe, it was a remarkable waste for God to create so many other, lifeless galaxies. Yet any talk of waste gives the impression that God is somehow scrambling around in the heavens with limited resources and that He should therefore have been more sparing in His creation. The biblical teaching, though, is that God simply spoke matter into existence; He had no limits or constraints upon His creation. In fact, such reasoning on the part of man simply highlights man's arrogance in thinking that he can understand God's thoughts. In the Bible, God confronts a man called Job for his lack of understanding with these words:

Where were you when I laid the foundation of the earth?
Tell me, if you have understanding.
Who determined its measurements—surely you
know! . . .
Have you entered into the springs of the sea,
or walked in the recesses of the deep?
Have the gates of death been revealed to you,
or have you seen the gates of deep darkness?
Have you comprehended the expanse of the earth?
Declare, if you know all this . . .

Do you know the ordinances of the heavens?
  Can you establish their rule on the earth?

(Job 38:4–5, 16–18, 33)

The sheer size of the heavens should actually remind us that we are not as smart as we think we are! God says in Isaiah, 'For as the heavens are higher than the earth, so are my ways higher than your ways and my thoughts than your thoughts' (Isaiah 55:9). God's understanding is infinite; ours is not. Yet even with our limited understanding we have discovered many scientific reasons why the universe is the way it is. The precise fine-tuning detectable in the universe, reliant upon hundreds of different physical constants, indicates that the earth is placed in the precise location that makes it capable of supporting life.[7]

Finally, we often see that God uses the vastness of the universe to teach us important theological truths about Himself, such as the measure of His love for us and the certainty of His promises:

For as high as the heavens are above the earth,
  so great is his steadfast love towards those who fear him;
as far as the east is from the west,
  so far does he remove our transgressions from us.

(Psalm 103:11–12)

Thus says the LORD,
who gives the sun for light by day
  and the fixed order of the moon and the stars for light by night,
who stirs up the sea so that its waves roar—
  the LORD of hosts is his name:
'If this fixed order departs
  from before me, declares the LORD,

then shall the offspring of Israel cease
  from being a nation before me for ever.'
Thus says the LORD:
'If the heavens above can be measured,
  and the foundations of the earth below can be explored,
then I will cast off all the offspring of Israel
  for all that they have done,
declares the LORD.'

(Jeremiah 31:35–37)

So, far from being a source of feelings of insignificance, the vast universe is actually a constant reminder every day and every night of God's great love and faithfulness. Surely this is what the psalmist meant when he said, 'The heavens declare the glory of God, and the sky above proclaims his handiwork. Day to day pours out speech, and night to night reveals knowledge.'

Why have I spent so long on this point, and how does this help you to understand who you are as an individual? Quite simply it's because, as you search to understand who you are, if your starting point is wrong, any and every conclusion that you draw will also be wrong—or, at best, incomplete. As we shall see in the next chapter, an incorrect starting point can have terrible consequences.

Notes

1 Modern text, William Shakespeare, *King Lear*, Act 1, Scene 4, 'King Lear Translation', SparkNotes, http://nfs.sparknotes.com/lear/page_64.html.

2 'Richard Dawkins and Ricky Gervais on Religion', YouTube, 30 December 2012, https://www.youtube.com/watch?v=nflBEJYZG7o.

3 'Day 4: Lunar Orbit 9', Apollo 8, Apollo Flight Journal, https://history.nasa.gov/afj/ap08fj/21day4_orbit9.html.

4 Carl Sagan, *Pale Blue Dot: A Vision of the Human Future in Space* (New York: Random House, 1994), pp. 6–7.

5 'Gloria Patri', Wikipedia, https://en.wikipedia.org/wiki/Gloria_Patri.

6 Quoted in Nancy Pearcy, 'Design and the Discriminating Public: Gaining a Hearing from Ordinary People', in W. A. Dembski and J. M. Kushiner (eds), *Signs of Intelligence: Understanding the Intelligent Design* (Grand Rapids: Brazos, 2001), p. 46.

7 For more information about anthropic constants, see John Barrow and Frank Tipler, *The Anthropic Cosmological Principle* (Oxford: Oxford University Press, 1988).

3 Mirror, mirror, on the wall

The ability of fairy tales to captivate and enchant audiences both young and old is no doubt the reason for their longevity. With heroes and villains, wicked witches, damsels in distress, handsome princes and an array of other mythical creatures, these folkloric tales have been retold down through the ages to the delight of many. Certainly, Hollywood has stirred our imagination through classic retellings and modern adaptations. One of the most famous fairy tales worldwide is the story of Snow White, immortalized by the original Disney adaptation and loved by children across the globe.

In this fairy tale there is a wicked queen, beautiful, but proud and arrogant. She possessed a magic mirror, and every morning she would stand before it and say:

Mirror, mirror, on the wall,
Who in this land is fairest of all?

To which the mirror would respond, 'You, my queen, are fairest of all.' The queen would then be content that the mirror had told the truth and that her identity as the most beautiful woman in the land had been confirmed.

The story continues that as Snow White grew up she became beautiful, even more so than the wicked queen. So one day, when the queen asked her mirror the usual question, the mirror answered:

You, my queen, are fair; it is true.
But Snow White is a thousand times fairer than you.[1]

On hearing this statement, the queen's heart was so overcome with envy and pride that she could not stand the sight of Snow White and began to plot her demise.

CHOOSE YOUR MIRROR WISELY

In some way we can all relate to the queen because we all have our 'mirrors' that we use to tell us who we are. When we look in a mirror we see our reflection and we make judgements about ourselves, and usually the 'mirrors' we use are the opinions of the world and of those around us. Just like the queen in Snow White we have come to crave that affirmation from the 'mirror'. In a culture of airbrushed magazine covers a false image of beauty has been exalted that is impossible to compete with. Yet just as the queen would ask the mirror how beautiful she was, many people today ask their smartphones how 'beautiful' they are. They eagerly wait and watch to see who 'likes' their photos, sometimes even inviting opinions on social media with phrases such as 'hot or not', 'like for comment' or 'rate me', in order to make the 'mirror' speak.

For many, this may seem trivial, but for others it is more serious; they have become obsessed with self-image and trying to match the world's sexualized standards of beauty. It is reminiscent of Narcissus in Greek mythology, who was celebrated for his beauty and had many admirers. He eventually fell in love with his own image reflected in a pool. After gazing endlessly at his reflection, despair and remorse overcame him, and he took his own life. As with

Narcissus, this obsession to meet an unobtainable standard has left many people insecure, empty and broken, constantly seeking affirmation from others. A world which rejects God will always take something that is beautiful and twist it into something it was never meant to be. The objectification and over-sexualization in our culture is devastating. The gift of sex that God made so sacred, which represents perhaps the highest form of intimacy possible between two people—a union which bonds them together for life, to share and be completely submitted to one another; a bond that is so sacred it had to be protected by a covenant, namely marriage—all this has been de-sacralized to the point where it is reduced to nothing more than physical satisfaction.

Truly we live in the world which was envisaged by the Marquis de Sade. It is from his name that we get the term 'sadism', the notion of gaining sexual satisfaction through inflicting pain. The Marquis de Sade was an eighteenth-century French aristocrat who was well known for all manner of debauchery, so the term we derive from his name is well deserved. He considered sexual gratification, by any means, to be simply another commodity in the marketplace. As a result, in his view, people operated merely as a means to fulfil personal sexual desires. Any moral significance was removed, and sexual pleasure was viewed as something which ethically had no more significance than a trip to the shops or eating dinner. Is this not the world in which we live today—one where sexual satisfaction is exalted to the highest place on the pedestal, where TV shows regularly portray love as simply fulfilling sexual desire?

THE SEXUAL REVOLUTION

But the world thinks that this is OK. Pornography and prostitution are among the largest industries in the world today, and every sort of sexual deviancy is available at the click of a button. We are only beginning to see the effects of this across culture as addiction to pornography is becoming rampant and the push for sexualization begins at younger and younger ages. The phenomenon of 'dating' apps such as Tinder has caused de Sade's world of commodity sex to be realized. *Vanity Fair* magazine described the advent of Tinder as the 'dating apocalypse'.[2] It is an app that people use basically to arrange casual sex dates by simply swiping through photos of other users and contacting the ones they like. There are even apps designed to help married people have affairs! Those who seek to maintain some sacredness and exclusivity to their sexuality not only must resist the social pressure to be promiscuous and the temptation from the surplus of sexual imagery available, but will also be mocked as relics of a bygone repressed era, on the wrong side of history.

On the one hand, the world has tried its best to devalue the meaning of sex so that it can be entered into freely and without consequence—it is simply a longing that must be satisfied—but, on the other hand, there exists a more troubling side to this image reflected upon us by the mirror of the age. Professor Carl R. Trueman has summarized it well:

> There is another force at play today which seems to be in conflict with the above: The belief that our sexual desires determine who we are at the deepest level. This is somewhat ironic: The age which denies any real significance to sex also wants to argue that sexual

desires are of paramount importance to personal identity and fulfillment. Squaring that particular circle will no doubt generate a whole textbook full of neuroses in the coming years.[3]

Thus, the sexual revolution takes away with one hand what it purports to give with the other. It claims to offer free love (sex) with no consequences, but it can only offer this by reducing people to mere instruments for one another's sexual fulfilment. But to market this successfully to the public it pushes the lie that a person's sexual desires are a pivotal part of their identity, vital to understanding who they are. Somehow fulfilling sexual desires is made to be the pinnacle of true personhood, the ultimate expression of just 'being true to who you are'. Yet how can this be if these 'desires' have already been evacuated of all meaning and significance, so that they are no different from selecting a dinner preference on a menu?

To limit the richness of human identity to mere sexual gratification is actually to sow the seeds for a society's cultural demise. When that which should be sacred is made cheap, when adult desire is placed above its proper place, when a culture loses the ability to make moral judgements and promotes practices which are harmful to the next generation, that society will crumble under the weight of its own lack of restraint. Consider the words of Alfred Edersheim, a scholar who made an extensive study of the cultural environment of first-century Judaism, in his description of Roman society in the first century:

It has been rightly said, that the idea of conscience, as we understand it, was unknown to heathenism. Absolute right did not

> exist. Might was right. The social relations exhibited, if possible, even deeper corruption. The sanctity of marriage had ceased. Female dissipation and the general dissoluteness led at last to an almost entire cessation of marriage. Abortion, and the exposure and murder of newly-born children, were common and tolerated; unnatural vices, which even the greatest philosophers practiced, if not advocated, attained proportions which defy description.[4]

This description could easily fit a number of the so-called 'civilized' societies today. They have rejected absolute truth, for we define our own truth, and 'morals' are all relative to the individual. This has led to extreme sexual promiscuity that damages the structure of the family and leads to the murder of children. It is into this culture that the message of Jesus comes with stark relevance—a message of hope and salvation, a true foundation for equality of persons. It offers a worldview that affirms the value and dignity of all people as created beings, affirming that life is sacred, and telling people that their true identities are to be found in their relationship with God. The Christian teaching is that marriage is sacred, that children are a blessing, and that wives are to be honoured, cherished and loved above all else. This is the seed of a real revolution!

By and large, Roman society rejected the message of Christ, and despite being one of the strongest empires ever to exist, and one that exerted such lasting influence on Western civilization, Rome itself fell to the Barbarians and into the annals of history.

ANOTHER VIEW FROM THE MIRROR

Although the issue of sexual identity is one way in which the truth is twisted and offered to our culture, there is perhaps an even more fundamental issue that impacts the question of who we are. It is the question of where we came from: our origins. This issue is very important to the subject of this book, so it is worth examining in a little more detail.

By far the most pervasive answer in our culture today to the question of human origins comes from evolutionary biology. The 'General Theory of Evolution' (GTE) states that 'all the living forms in the world have arisen from a single source which itself came from an inorganic form'.[5] The history of evolutionary theory is a large and complex subject, but we can trace the modern account to a man named Charles Darwin. His legacy was to posit a specific mechanism that could explain the origin of species, a mechanism he called 'natural selection'. Strictly, he was not the first to come up with this idea, but his book *On the Origin of Species* popularized the theory beyond anything previously written. Modern Darwinists, taking insights from the work of geneticist Gregor Mendel, updated Darwin's theory by arguing that random genetic mutations were the means by which natural selection conserved the beneficial mutations to produce new species. This is known as Neo-Darwinian evolution, and it is this particular system of thought that dominates not only the scientific establishment but also popular culture.

DARWINIAN OPTIONS

It is not the purpose of this book to delve into the specifics of the debate surrounding the validity of the Darwinian model, but the implications do radically impact the subject of human identity which we are examining. There is a problem that needs to be brought out into the open first: although much of this evolutionary teaching is couched in supposedly objective scientific language, lurking beneath it exists a prior commitment to philosophical naturalism. This is the view mentioned earlier: that the universe is a closed system consisting only of the material world. This means that the actual *modus operandi* of those committed to philosophical naturalism rules out of the game any evidence for God, the soul or the immaterial. This really means that something like Darwinism must be true regardless of the evidence for or against it. All subsequent investigations are then conducted in line with this starting philosophical assumption. Anyone who believes in a naturalistic universe must, therefore, believe in evolution. Tom Bethel explains, 'He "knows" that it is true, not because he sees it in the genes, or in the lab, or in the fossils, but because it is embedded in his philosophy.'[6]

On this view, then, the development of all species is attributed to an unguided natural process with no deeper meaning or purpose: just time, matter, death and chance. Any evidence that seems to indicate something to the contrary is referred back to the naturalistic starting assumption and reinterpreted through the grid of naturalism. This may sound like religious scaremongering, but it is actually a point that many evolutionists themselves will admit. Richard Dawkins, one of the best-known naturalist professors today, says that, 'even if there were no actual evidence in favour of Darwinian Theory . . . we should still be justified in preferring it over all rival theories'.[7] Even blunter is Scott Todd, a Kansas State University professor, who wrote in the science journal *Nature* that, 'even if all the data points to an intelligent designer, such a hypothesis is excluded from science because it is not naturalistic'.[8]

Cleary there is a philosophical commitment at play here. This is why Dawkins can say that biology 'is the study of complicated things that give the appearance of having been designed for a purpose', then immediately proclaim that 'the only watch maker in nature is the blind forces of physics'.[9] One is reminded of the humorous duck test: if it looks like a duck, swims like a duck and quack likes a duck, then it probably is a duck—unless, of course, you have already ruled out the possibility of it being a duck before you observe these features, in which case it must be something else. The parallel seems clear, which is why you find someone as eminent as Francis Crick, co-discoverer of the structure of DNA, giving this little piece of advice: 'Biologists must constantly keep in mind that what they see was not designed, but rather evolved.'[10]

WHAT DOES THIS MEAN FOR HUMAN IDENTITY?

Darwinism attributes all the diversity of life to solely natural causes. In effect, the words of Genesis, 'In the beginning, God', have been replaced with, 'In the beginning were the particles'.[11] Which mechanism provides the best explanation for the complexity and diversity of life, mind or matter is not the issue, but only whether the proposal offered is naturalistic. God has been evicted. This is what Richard Dawkins meant when he said that Darwinism allows him to be 'an intellectually fulfilled atheist'.[12]

So what are the implications of this naturalistic worldview for our lives? They are quite considerable. They have more impact coming from the words of those who hold to this view. For example, consider carefully to the words of Princeton ethicist Peter Singer: 'Life as a whole had no meaning. Life began, as the best available theories tell us, in a chance combination of molecules; it then evolved through random mutations and natural selection. All this just happened; it did not happen for any purpose.'[13] Notice that he says 'the best available theories'. What he is really saying is that the best available naturalistic theories force us to the conclusion that our lives have no purpose and no meaning; this is a high price to pay for the desire to evict God.

In extremely honest words Richard Dawkins also provides support for a meaningless universe:

> In a universe of blind physical forces and genetic replication, some people are going to get hurt, other people are going to get lucky and you won't find any rhyme or reason in it, nor any justice. The universe we observe has precisely the properties we should expect if there is, at the bottom, no design, no purpose, no evil, no good. Nothing but blind, pitiless, indifference. DNA neither knows nor cares. DNA just is. And we dance to its music.[14]

Dawkins is being dreadfully consistent here. If life is a result of blind physical forces and evolution, then the logical conclusion is that there is no meaning to life and no foundation for ethics. This is a frightening reality. Yet, at the same time, neither Richard Dawkins nor the most hardened naturalist actually lives in accordance with this belief. They are compelled to believe in moral constructs such as good and evil and justice in order to navigate through life. The forced inconsistency is revealing because it indicates that the naturalistic worldview and the evolutionary model for the origins of man cannot account for the whole of reality as we experience it. This means there must be a problem! As the above quote shows, these issues intersect with many areas of our lives: compassion, suffering, ethics, justice, purpose, meaning, evil and good. All of these things are connected to the question of who we are.

OUR ANCESTRY

To mark the tenth anniversary of the first draft of the Human Genome Project in 2013 the London Science Museum opened a new interactive exhibition called 'Who Am I?' The exhibition is structured around four zones that invite you to explore the science of who you are. The zones are called 'I am my body', 'I am human', 'I am my family' and 'I am more than myself'. Although the video introduction admits that 'no one can really define what it means to be human', it quite confidently asserts, 'your brain holds the answers'. The exhibition is primarily an interactive one, seemingly aimed at the many schools which visit the museum, but it nevertheless believes that all the answers are to be found in the natural world—that is, in our brains, our genes (ancestry) and our DNA.

So what identity does Darwinism give us? In this view the human being is nothing more than a highly evolved primate. Our existence is a mere accident, the outcome of time, chance and natural selection. Mankind holds no privileged position in the universe. As the late Stephen J. Gould, a world-leading evolutionary biologist, wrote, humans are a 'tiny and accidental evolutionary twig . . . a little mammalian afterthought with a curious evolutionary invention' called the human brain.[15] How's that for an answer? You're nothing but a small insignificant 'mammalian afterthought'!

One of the reasons why this topic is such a contentious issue is not, as it is often presented, because one side has a mountain of evidence and the other side has very little. In fact, both sides have exactly the same evidence. It is just that the evidence is interpreted in two different ways—that is, according to two different starting assumptions: naturalism or supernaturalism. This is the real issue: is God obligatory or not?

Although many try to claim there is no conflict between evolution and theism, the majority of leading evolutionary scientists reject attempts at harmonization, claiming instead that the two are in direct opposition. Darwin's theory of natural selection 'provided a naturalistic account of the origin of species—an explanation for design without a designer'.[16] It is simply not consistent to hold the belief that two entirely contradictory accounts of life's origins can be true at the same time. It was either God or an entirely natural process. One replaces the other.

DIFFERENT STARTING POINTS

This substitute of evolution as the creative agent rather than God is graphically yet subtly illustrated on the Smithsonian Museum of Natural History website, Human Origins. Under the section entitled 'What does It Mean to Be Human?' it says that 'part of what it means to be human is how we became human'. This phrase is placed below a large picture of a human hand being outstretched to reach an outstretched chimpanzee arm; the two fingers are nearly touching.[17] There is a subtle significance to this particular image. It recreates the famous Michelangelo painting *The Creation of Adam* that adorns the ceiling of the Sistine Chapel and features God reaching out his hand to touch and give life to his creation of the first man Adam. This image has become iconic of humanity and has long been imitated in popular culture. The poster for the 1982 movie *E.T. the Extra-Terrestrial* featured this same imagery.

Yet the Smithsonian image is revealing. The hand of God, which in the original fresco is on the right-hand side, has been replaced with the hand of the ape. The symbolism of the original is that God created man in his image, but the museum picture now says that man has been 'created' by the primate ancestor from which we evolved. This is subtle but powerful imagery which clearly illustrates different starting points for these two views of human origins.

This worldview shift that occurred with the Darwinian revolution is deeply connected to the question of who we are and how we live our lives. The naturalistic story has a number of rather distressing implications. Think about the following words of Nobel Laureate Professor Steven Weinberg:

> Not only do we not find any point to life laid out for us in nature, no objective basis for our moral principles, no correspondence between what we think is the moral law and the laws of nature . . . the emotions that we most treasure, our love for our wives and husbands and children, are made possible by chemical processes in our brains that are what they are as a result of natural selection acting on chance mutations over millions of years. And yet we must not sink into nihilism or stifle our emotions. At our best we live on a knife-edge, between wishful thinking on one hand and, on

> the other, despair. Living without God isn't easy. But its very difficulty offers one other consolation—that there is a certain honour, or perhaps just a grim satisfaction, in facing up to our condition without despair and without wishful thinking—with good humour, but without God.[18]

If you still do not grasp the magnitude of this topic, read that quote again and consider the statements carefully. Once again, we see that the cost of evicting God is too high: it leaves us living a life full of contradictions.

THE ROTTEN FRUIT FROM THE TREE OF LIFE

The notion that man is simply an evolved animal has, at various times in history, led to the dignity of mankind being defaced by our own actions. Darwin's 'tree of life' proposed that all species originated from a primordial life form which itself originated from a 'warm little pond'.[19] From this first life came all the diversity we see today. The famous tree of life image which Darwin first drew in 1837 has been commonplace in almost all biology textbooks to this day. Although the tree concept has been seriously disputed among scientists, it is so entrenched within the evolutionary model that attempts to fully uproot it have proven difficult. In 2009 the magazine *New Scientist* published an article entitled 'Uprooting Darwin's Tree'[20] which dealt with the controversy surrounding the evolutionary tree. The article was not well received, with the editor receiving many letters expressing outrage that one of their own would dare to question this icon of evolution.

So the family tree of life is still central to the theory of evolution today, especially the evolution of humans. At the bottom of the tree are the branches that take us through the earliest stages of human evolution. The typical tree (as seen on the Smithsonian human origins display[21]) moves from our supposed earliest human ancestors, the *Ardipithecus* group, to the *Australopithicus* group, up through the *Paranthropus* group and finally into the *Homo* group, which is where we find *Homo sapiens*. This information is more popularly presented in a typical textbook as a horizontal ape-to-man chart. We have all seen these charts where, on the left, we start with an ape-like creature or 'ape-man', who gradually progresses by becoming more upright, until we reach a full human at the end on the right. The image gives the impression that clear fossil evidence exists for all of these stages of human evolution. In reality, the chart is grossly misleading. Usually the first couple of images are simply of extinct quadrupeds who would not have been bipedal. Also, *Homo erectus* was a fully formed human, so the chart relies heavily on the artist's impression to give it the crude cave-men-like features.

Actually, the neat and tidy progression from ape to human represented in the chart is nothing of the sort, a fact that even some evolutionists will admit:

> There is a popular image of human evolution that you'll find all over the place . . . on the left of the picture there's an ape . . . on the right, a man . . . between the two is a succession of figures that become ever more like humans . . . Our progress from ape to human looks so smooth, so tidy. It's such a beguiling image that even the experts are loath to let it go. But it is an illusion.[22]

Another troubling issue that arises from these typical monkey-to-man charts is that the majority of them will display the most evolved human specimen as a white man while the lesser-evolved images get progressively darker skinned. The image seems to imply that dark-skinned humans are less evolved than paler, 'white'-skinned humans. Immediately, one can sense the outrage from evolutionists for even implying such a suggestion: 'It is simply the fact that the original primates were darker so there is a natural progression through evolution,' they might respond. But let's be clear: while I am definitely not saying that all those who believe in evolution are racist, I am saying that evolutionary theory has in the past contributed to a number of the most racist ideologies in history, by providing them with a seemingly scientific justification.

Evolution did not create racism, but it has definitely contributed to it. The late leading evolutionist Stephen J. Gould admitted that 'biological arguments for racism may have been common before 1859, but they increased by orders of magnitude following the acceptance of evolutionary theory'.[23] I find it interesting that in a racially sensitive culture like ours, in which TV personalities can be lambasted via social media or even fired for making comments that merely hint of racism, we still give evolution a free pass, promoting it at every turn. This 'sacred' belief must be protected at all costs. Why? Simply because the only other alternative is . . . God!

DARWIN'S BOOKS

Some may protest that Darwin was simply a product of his time, so he mirrored his culture's views on race. However, when we consult the works of Charles Darwin, we find a very explicit theory of race which cannot be excused as a mere cultural expression; rather, it is a direct and logical conclusion based upon his theory of evolution. The actual full title of Darwin's 1859 book was *On the Origin of Species: The Preservation of Favoured Races and the Struggle for Life*. Today the subtitle is usually omitted, as mention of favoured races is a bit unsettling, yet this concept is inherent to the theory itself. It is true that, in *Origin of Species*, Darwin was not really addressing the issue of human evolution but rather the evolution of animals. He did, however, write another book in 1871, *The Descent of Man*, which directly applied evolutionary theory to humans. In this book we clearly see the concept of lower races and higher races being popularized.

In *The Descent of Man* Darwin writes, 'The sole object of this work is to consider, firstly, whether man, like every other species, is descended from some pre-existing form; secondly, the manner of his development; and thirdly, the value of the differences between the so-called races of man.'[24] Darwin applied his theory of natural selection, or survival of the fittest, to humanity. He predicted that the outcome would be that 'the civilised races of man will almost certainly exterminate, and replace throughout the world, the savage races . . . The break between man and his nearest allies will be wider, . . . instead of now between the negro or the Australian (aboriginal) and the gorilla.'[25]

Giving such a belief widespread scientific respectability led to man committing unthinkable crimes against humanity. Shortly after the publication of *Origin of Species*, many Australian aboriginals were murdered by European scientists so that their body parts could be used for museum displays of supposed evolutionary 'missing links'. Such horror was sanitized by the evolutionary understanding that these people were a 'sub-species' and thus not fully developed humans. It was due to the evolutionary model that they were doomed to extinction as the weaker race via the process of *assisting* 'natural selection'.

Evolution rejects the concept that all humans are made in the image of God with equal dignity and honour. Once this concept is rejected there remains no safeguard for those who have been classified as lower races. Even a secular Australian historian wrote that, 'in earlier periods, one of the few persistent barriers to the social Darwinist theory in Australia was the Christian doctrine that all human beings were of 'one blood'.[26]

SOCIAL DARWINISM AND EUGENICS

It is not hard to see why culture accepted the idea that there were lower (less evolved) and higher (more evolved) races when the theory was given scientific justification by the academic establishment. What Darwin wrote in *The Descent of Man* was just the beginning. It was not long before the social implications of Darwinism seeped into the world. A man named Herbert Spencer, a prominent disciple of Darwin and the one who actually coined the term 'survival of the fittest', was the first to radically apply the principles of Darwinism to human society, and with this he became the father of social Darwinism. The concept is relatively straightforward. The whole of human society is seen as a product of evolution. Therefore, the stronger societies or nations will flourish and the weaker people in society will be eliminated. In this theory, stronger nations basically have the right to do whatever they want to weaker nations, as they deserve their place at the top—evolution has placed them there. Herbert Spencer opposed any social support for the less fit in society, such as benefits, medical care and education. He wrote, 'A nation which fosters its good-for-nothings will end by becoming a good-for-nothing nation.'[27] The practical outworking of such a social theory has devastating potential. And to be sure, it was not long before social Darwinism was being directly applied to a new and flourishing field known as eugenics.

Eugenics is a pseudo-scientific attempt to improve the physical and mental characteristics of the human race by effectively culling the 'unfit' from the genetic pool. Amazingly, it was none other than Charles Darwin's cousin Francis Galton who pioneered this movement, coining the term 'eugenics' in 1883. The word 'eugenics' is composed of two Greek words meaning 'well' and 'born'[28] and indicates a scientific attempt to perpetuate the positive qualities found in humanity by selective breeding, and conversely, to eradicate any negative traits by whichever means are most effective. It is natural selection in action—with a little help from the men in lab coats.

This concept—that race can be improved via genetic manipulation—is firmly rooted in Darwinian soil, as the *Encyclopedia of Bioethics* makes clear: 'The emergence of interest in eugenics during that century had multiple roots. The most important was the theory of evolution, for Francis Galton's ideas on eugenics . . . were a direct logical outgrowth of the scientific doctrine elaborated by his cousin, Charles Darwin.'[29]

Selection stands at the very heart of Darwinian theory, and if humans are simply the result of evolution, not significantly different from the animals, why should the process have stopped with us? The underlying theory of eugenics was that it should not, and that efforts need to be made to help direct this process in order to produce a genetically and mentally superior race of humans. Such a theory of humanity destroys any foundation for the notion that 'all men are created equal'. Although, historically, this has been the ideology of Western nations, evolutionary theory leaves no room for the concept of man being created in the image of God. Unless human beings bear God's image, there is no reason why they would possess a unique dignity, different from the animals. There would be no concept of grace, forgiveness or redemption, and no understanding of sin or evil—all negative traits are hereditary results and must be eliminated from the gene pool!

Unfortunately, this was not merely a theoretical problem. In the late nineteenth and early twentieth centuries the practical fruits of social Darwinism became evident. In America, the large influx of immigration during this period, and the challenges this brought to the existing demographic, caused scientists to propose using eugenics as the solution. The idea was to encourage the superior (white) humans to produce larger families, while simultaneously restricting the size of the 'inferior' humans. Those deemed 'unfit'—which included people with disabilities, those with epilepsy, the poor, the blind, the deaf, those with certain diseases, or just criminals and drug addicts—were subjected to forced sterilization and even euthanasia to prevent undesirable breeding and further pollution of racial purity.

EUGENICS AND NAZI GERMANY

The Darwinian revolution spread rapidly throughout Germany, due in part to the relentless proselytizing of men like Ernst Haeckel. Haeckel, a highly respected zoology professor, was one of Darwin's most devoted disciples in Germany; he was responsible for the first German translation of Darwin's book *Origin of Species*. An avid popularizer of evolutionary theory, Haeckel was so zealous for Darwin's ideas that he was happy to fraudulently produce 'evidence' to bolster the theory. The fraud he is most famous for is his doctored embryo drawings which he used to 'prove' his idea of embryonic recapitulation. This was the idea that the human embryo goes through (recapitulates) different stages of our alleged evolutionary history so that, at certain stages of development, it has gills like a fish and a tail like a monkey. This is known as the principle that 'ontogeny recapitulates phylogeny'. Although his drawings are often still circulated, it is now known that this theory is entirely wrong and the evidence he provided with his embryo illustrations was fake.

Despite this, Ernst Haeckel became one of Germany's leading scientists, promoting his theories to the academic establishment as well as to the common man. This meant that he was inordinately successful at ensuring that people adopted the Darwinian account of human origins along with his own ideas of racial superiority and support for social Darwinism. His efforts were responsible for persuading his countrymen to 'accept their evolutionary destiny as a "master race" and "outcompete" inferior peoples, since it was right and natural that only the "fittest" should survive'.[30]

Haeckel's views on race soon became German policy, which entailed the belief that the Indo-Germanic race sat at the top of the evolutionary tree. He considered people with dark skin to be 'incapable of a true inner culture and of a higher mental development'. He even went on to say that these so-called lower races were 'psychologically nearer to the mammals (apes and dogs) than to civilized Europeans' and that 'we must, therefore, assign a totally different value to their lives'.[31]

This teaching contributed to the tragic events that followed in Germany. Stephen J. Gould wrote this about Haeckel:

> His greatest influence was, ultimately, in another direction—National Socialism (Nazism). His evolutionary racism; his call to the German people for racial purity and unflinching devotion to . . . his belief that harsh, inexorable laws of evolution ruled human civilisation and nature alike, conferring upon favoured races the right to dominate others . . . all contributed to the rise of Nazism.[32]

It was Haeckel's version of Darwinism that was incorporated into Adolf Hitler's book *Mein Kampf* (1925), which means 'my struggle', a phrase taken from Haeckel's translation of Darwin's phrase 'the struggle for existence'. Adolph Hitler was a committed Darwinist, and one of the central tenets of the Nazi party was that the Darwinian 'struggle for existence governed all beings'.[33] Racial superiority was pivotal in Hitler's vision for the development of a 'superior race', a concept already well established and accepted by Darwinian scientists and eugenicists across the globe. The stronger races should suppress and dominate the inferior ones, not permitting the latter to mix with those who were racially superior. Hitler believed that any mixing of racial boundaries was a disgrace and would hinder the process of producing a higher level of evolutionary advanced humans—the Master Race. Hitler accused those of 'inferior' races (e.g. Jews and Slavs) of trying to 'ruin the white-haired race' by defiling the pure blood lines of the Aryans in an attempt to systematically 'lower the racial level by a continuous poisoning of individuals'.[34]

Hitler applied these social Darwinist principles to his governmental policies, as reflected in the Nuremberg Laws, to prevent pollution of the Aryan race. Hitler's policies enacted a government which was actively seeking to apply the concept of 'survival of the fittest' to mankind and would thus entail the government-assisted elimination of all inferior species which could hinder the upward human evolutionary process. Tragically, this concern led to the development of his Final Solution, the systematic extermination of over six million Jews and over five million Poles, Slavs and gypsies because the German scientists of the day had deemed them 'inferior'.

This tragic episode in history illustrates clearly that if we begin with an incorrect starting point in the search for identity, we can end up very far from the truth. The issue of origins is extremely important in considering the question of what it means to be human. The view that we arrived here through a process of death, time and chance affords mankind a very different status from the view of special creation.

Consider the words of Victor Frankl, a leading neurologist

and psychiatrist who lost all but one member of his family to the Holocaust. He survived three different concentration camps:

> If we present man with a concept of man which is not true, we may well corrupt him. When we present man as an automaton of reflexes, as a mind machine, as a bundle of instincts, as a pawn of drives and reactions, as a mere product of instinct, hereditary and environment, we feed the nihilism to which modern man is, in any case prone.

This is exactly what I have tried to illustrate: that Darwinian theory presents man with a concept that is not true, and that, historically, this has contributed to a corrupt view of humanity. Frankl continues:

> I became acquainted with the last stage of that corruption in my second concentration camp, Auschwitz. The gas chambers of Auschwitz were the ultimate consequence of the theory that man is nothing more than the product of heredity and environment—or as the Nazis liked to say, of 'blood and soil'. I am absolutely convinced that the gas chambers of Auschwitz, Treblinka and Majdanek were ultimately prepared not in some Ministry or other in Berlin, but rather at the desks and in the lecture halls of nihilistic scientists and philosophers.[35]

The old adage 'Ideas have consequences' is true. One of the many philosophies that contributed to this tragic period of history was Darwinian evolution. The acceptance of Darwinian thought paved the way for the devaluing of human life and the eventual elimination of those who were deemed less human. Such a worldview or philosophy stands in direct contradiction to the biblical concept that man is created in the image of God and that all people are therefore 'created equal'.

When it comes to answering the question 'Who am I?', we begin either with the philosophies of men or with the Word of God. The apostle Paul warns his readers to see 'that no one takes you captive by philosophy and empty deceit, according to human tradition, according to the elemental spirits of the world, and not according to Christ' (Colossians 2:8). This is where the battle has always been. It is not about evidence, not about fossils or science, but about authority: do we accept God's authority, or do we elevate man to the position of God? Man is still struggling to answer the question of who we are, but God's answer has been consistent from the beginning. If only we would listen!

A VIEW FROM A DIFFERENT MIRROR

Having looked at the answers offered by the world to the question of what it means to be human, it is now time to turn our attention to God's answer. We are told in the book of James that the Bible itself is like a mirror; it gives us a description of our identity as God intended:

> But be doers of the word, and not hearers only, deceiving yourselves. For if anyone is a hearer of the word and not a doer, he is like a man who looks intently at his natural face in a mirror. For he looks at himself and goes away and at once forgets what he was like. But the one who looks into the perfect law, the law of liberty, and perseveres, being no hearer who forgets but a doer who acts, he will be blessed in his doing. (James 1:22–25)

This description is not affected by whatever cultural expression is in vogue, nor is it interested in whatever false identity you may have assumed for yourself. This identity is perfect, gleaned from a perfect law, and it is this identity we should require. The sixteenth-century Reformer John Calvin said that a person 'may see himself as he really is by looking into the faithful mirror of scripture'.[36]

NOTES OVERLEAF ➡

Notes

1 Jacob and Wilhelm Grimm, 'Little Snow-White', http://www.pitt.edu/~dash/grimm053.html.

2 Nancy Jo Sales, 'Tinder and the Dawn of the "Dating Apocalypse"', *Vanity Fair*, 6 August 2015, http://www.vanityfair.com/culture/2015/08/tinder-hook-up-culture-end-of-dating.

3 Carl R. Trueman, 'We're All Sadists Now', *First Things*, 13 August 2015, http://www.firstthings.com/blogs/firstthoughts/2015/08/were-all-sadists-now.

4 Alfred Edersheim, *The Life and Times of Jesus the Messiah: Complete and Unabridged in One Volume* (Peabody, MA: Hendrickson, 2002), p. 179.

5 G. A. Kerkut (1927–2004), *Implications of Evolution* (Oxford: Pergamon, 1960), p. 157.

6 Tom Bethell, 'Against Sociobiology', *First Things*, January 2001, https://www.firstthings.com/article/2001/01/against-sociobiology.

7 Richard Dawkins, *The Blind Watchmaker* (New York: Norton, 1986), p. 287.

8 S. C. Todd, correspondence to *Nature* 401, no. 6752 (30 Sept. 1999): 423.

9 Dawkins, *Blind Watchmaker,* pp. 1–5.

10 F. Crick, *What Mad Pursuit: A Personal View of Scientific Discovery* (London: Sloan Foundation Science, 1988), p. 138.

11 Phillip E. Johnson, *The Wedge of Truth: Splitting the Foundations of Naturalism* (Downers Grove, IL: InterVarsity Press, 2000), p. 155.

12 Dawkins, *Blind Watchmaker*, p. 6.

13 Peter Singer, *Practical Ethics*, 2nd edn (Cambridge: Cambridge University Press, 1993, repr. 1999), p. 331.

14 Richard Dawkins, *River out of Eden* (London: Weidenfeld & Nicholson, 1995), p. 133.

15 Stephen Jay Gould, *Bully for Brontosaurus* (New York: W. W. Norton, 1991), p. 13.

WHO AM I?

16 S. Stewart-Williams, 'Can an Evolutionist Believe in God?', *Philosophy Now* 47 (2004): 19.

17 See http://humanorigins.si.edu/.

18 S. Weinberg, 'Without God', *The New York Review of Books* 55, no. 14 (2008): 1.

19 F. Darwin, *The Life and Letters of Charles Darwin*, Vol. 2 (New York: Appleton & Co., 1911), pp. 202–203.

20 G. Lawnton, 'Uprooting Darwin's Tree', *New Scientist* 201, no. 2692 (2009): 34–39.

21 'Human Family Tree', Human Origins, http://humanorigins.si.edu/evidence/human-family-tree.

22 Bernard Wood, 'Who Are We?', *New Scientist* 176, no. 2366 (2002): 44–45.

23 Stephen Jay Gould, *Ontogeny and Phylogeny* (Cambridge, MA: Belknap-Harvard Press, 1977), pp. 127–128.

24 Charles Darwin, *The Descent of Man, and Selection in Relation to Sex* (London: John Murray, 1871), pp. 2–3.

25 Charles Darwin, *The Descent of Man, and Selection in Relation to Sex*, 2nd edn (London: John Murray, 1874), p. 178.

26 Joanna Cruickshank, 'Best of 2011: Darwin, Race and Religion in Australia', ABC Religion and Ethics, 9 January 2012, http://www.abc.net.au/religion/articles/2012/01/09/3187793.htm.

27 J. A. Thomson, *Herbert Spencer* (London: J. M. Dent & Co., 1906), p. 71.

28 F. Galton, *Inquiries into Human Faculty and Its Development* (London: J. M. Dent & Co., 1883), p. 138.

29 K. Ludmerer, 'Eugenics', in Mark Lappe (ed.), *Encyclopedia of Bioethics* (New York: The Free Press, 1978), p. 457.

30 Richard Milner, *The Encyclopedia of Evolution* (New York: Facts on File, 1990), p. 207.

31 Robert J. Lifton, *The Nazi Doctors: Medical Killing and the Psychology of Genocide* (New York: Basic, 1986), pp. 441–442.

32 Stephen Jay Gould, *Ontogeny and Phylogeny* (Cambridge, MA: Belknap-Harvard Press, 1977), pp. 77–78.

33 Christian Zentner and Friedemann Bedürftig (eds), *The Encyclopedia of the Third Reich* (New York: Da Capo Press, 1997), pp. 426–427.

34 Adolf Hitler, *Mein Kampf* (Cambridge: Houghton Mifflin/ Riverside Press, 1962), p. 325.

35 Viktor E. Frankl, *The Doctor and the Soul: From Psychotherapy to Logotherapy* (New York: Vintage, 1986), p. 27.

36 John Calvin, *Institutes of the Christian Religion,* trans. Henry Beveridge (North Charleston, SC: CreateSpace, 2015), 2.2.11, p. 174.

4 I am created

In this chapter we will examine some of the most important issues surrounding the identity of mankind. Due to their importance, and the ramifications that flow from them, it is necessary to examine them in some detail. The following story is designed to help us begin to consider them in an imaginative way.

2075 AD

In the year 2075 the world is a very different place. The planet's surface still lies ravaged from the great war of 2060. This war caused the death of half the world's population. During the final stages of the conflict, as populations decreased, smaller governments banded together with the hope of defeating each other. The fighting continued for ten years, until so few people remained who were willing to fight that one day it just seemed to stop. People called on the remaining governments to bring order. And order is what they brought. But order is not freedom.

The remaining powers merged to become the United Freedom Federation (UFF). The nation was divided up into county districts and a different judge placed as head of each county. At each judge's disposal is a regiment of UFF enforcers: dedicated soldiers whose lives are guided by their motto 'Maintain a free world for a free people'. Yet they have a very different interpretation of what constitutes a 'person'. The judicial department of the UFF has ruled that only those people who will improve the future of the free society they are building can become citizens of the Federation. The Federation has outlawed all religious belief, claiming that it is a 'virus of the mind', detrimental to the flourishing of human beings and highly contagious. Any non-citizens exhibiting such proclivities are to be immediately neutralized. Citizenship is refused to others for many reasons: sickness, age, disability, refusal to accept the Federation's Charter of Values, and for major infractions of district laws. Without citizenship you have no protection, no food, and no shelter within the safety of the district zones. Natural resources are scarce, and most technology was destroyed during the war. The only remaining source of power lies in the hands of the Federation.

Non-citizens, or 'strays', are forced to scavenge for a living amongst the ruins and in the forests outside county jurisdiction. Concerned that the number of 'strays' might become too large and upset the order of the counties, the UFF has done all in its power to dehumanize them. Citizens are constantly bombarded with UFF propaganda that describes strays as rabid animals and blames them for stealing precious resources that could be used to rebuild the world. This dehumanizing propaganda is made reputable by the UFF scientists, who provide citizens with enough 'evidence' to ease their consciences. In an attempt to rid the counties of strays, the UFF convened a council and launched the Human Control Division (HCD), simply known as 'selectors'. The HCD are tasked with controlling the number of strays and have been authorized to use whatever methods it deems appropriate in this task. They are ruthless and efficient in fulfilling their role. They have instituted annual culls during which HCD teams patrol areas outside the borders looking for camps of strays. If a camp is discovered, they round the people up; some are immediately eradicated, while others are prepared for transport and taken back to work camps, where they are forced to rebuild the infrastructure of the new developing world.

Strays live in constant fear of being found by the Human Control Division, comforting themselves with stories about cities of refuge outside the borders and of a resistance army that could lead them to freedom. Yet, until then, survival is the only goal.

My name is Chloe, and this is the story of the day they found us.

*****

'Run!' screamed Charlotte, her voice piercing the silence of the forest. She had been on watch through the night, and the intensity of her scream alerted the camp to our greatest fear—we had been discovered.

'Selectors! Run, run!' she screamed again. This threw the camp into panic. People scrambled around, not knowing what to do.

There were about forty of us who had gathered together, sheltering in the ruins of a dilapidated building deep within the forests of the Tragmor county district. There was little anyone could do as only those young enough to sprint stood a chance of escaping. Those who were aged and infirm huddled together in fear and waited for the guards to come. It was the end, and they knew it. Accepting defeat, they spent their last moments embracing those they loved.

I knew we had to try to run if we wanted to live.

I screamed for my sisters: 'Grace! Katie!'

'Chloe!' they shouted, as they ran towards me. 'What do we do?'

'Run!' I replied.

We turned and started to scramble over the hill, the adrenaline surging through our bodies as we pulled each other over the walls of the camp.

As we all began to run, we heard the sound of dogs barking all around us. The selectors had trained their dogs to hunt humans, and they were vicious beasts, capable of tearing a person to death if not called off.

We were too late. The silhouettes of the guards were emerging out of the forest from all directions, and the dogs were seconds away.

'Back down into the camp!' I said to my sisters; 'we have to hide.' It was our only chance, and it was a small chance.

At this point the dogs broke into the camp. They raced over the walls, their teeth exposed as they growled, lips curled, salivating at the prospect of human flesh.

People froze, not knowing in which direction to turn. The dogs spread out, almost as if they were surveying prospective meals. Two boys from our camp, George and Callum, turned to flee. The dogs immediately went for them.

'No!' screamed one of the young boys huddled with us.

The dogs were on them in seconds and sank their teeth into the calf muscles of the frightened boys. It was a manoeuvre the dogs had been trained for, designed to incapacitate someone so the guards could catch them.

'Aaarrghghhh!' the boys screamed in agony as the beasts brought them to the ground and began to shake them with great ferocity. The dogs wouldn't stop; the more the boys struggled, the deeper the beasts sank their teeth into the soft flesh.

There was loud weeping in the camp as people cowered in fear and lost all hope.

Then I saw them. The HCD guards came over the hill, dressed in their distinctive black uniforms. My heart pounded so fast that I could barely stand. I felt my sister's hand squeeze mine as tight as she could.

'Quick, follow me,' I said, and we turned and made our way to the house. It was a large, old timber-frame structure and we had played hide and seek in it many times with some of the children from the camp, so we knew where to hide. I directed my sisters to the basement, the best place to hide that we had found. I opened the trapdoor to the basement; it was a large hole in the ground, filled with cold mud and water at the bottom. I reassured them that they would be fine.

'No, Chloe, come with us,' they whispered, their lips quivering.

'I can't, we won't all fit. Hurry, we don't have long.' I knew that at any moment a guard could appear, and we would all be killed.

I lowered the trapdoor on top of them and covered it with dirt and leaves.

At that moment, I heard the door being kicked open as the guards entered the house. I could hear them laughing, taunting us, as they chanted, 'Come out, come out, wherever you are!' I knew one more place to hide: a gap between two walls which was just big enough for me. I crept across the hall and into the next room and squeezed into the hole between two old walls. I was well hidden, but I could see through the cracks in the timber outside into the camp.

I could see five guards.

'Enough!' shouted one of the guards. At his command the dogs stopped tearing apart the now lifeless bodies of the young boys, and sat to attention.

This guard was obviously in charge. He slowly roamed the perimeter while the other guards made the rest of the camp sit in a large circle. They looked so frightened—some weeping, some not moving, many with vacant expressions, unable to process what was happening.

'Sir,' said one of the guards addressing the captain, 'this is all of them. We lost a handful over the east hill into the forests, and we haven't cleared the house yet.'

'Send the hounds!' the captain growled furiously at the guard. He stepped closer, as if to intimate the young guard into obedience.

'I want them separated according to purpose. Look for signs of infection.' By this he meant any indication of religious belief.

'Those who are fit and can work, prepare for transport. Kill the rest!'

'Yes, sir,' replied the guard, clearly intimidated. He turned and signalled one of the guards to release the dogs.

The guard shouted 'Fetch! Kill!' and pointed towards the forest as the dogs ran off over the hill.

I breathed a sigh of relief as I saw the dogs run off; at least they wouldn't be used to search the house.

The members of the camp were ordered to strip. The guards walked around them, pulling off their clothing violently, sometimes swinging people to the ground before their garments ripped. They looked as if they were having fun.

'Captain,' shouted one of the guards suddenly, 'we have an infected one here.' This person was identified as infected because of the religious tattoos on his arm. The guards immediately sprang into action.

One guard approached with a long pole which had a noose on the end, and placed it over his neck. As he pulled it tight and turned him towards the captain, I could see the person's face. It was Rhys, one of our friends. I could see him choking for breath; his face was red and his hands were pulling at the cord tightening around his neck.

'Bring him here!' ordered the captain.

As the captain walked over he came very close to the wall where I was hiding. He was a large strong man and his face showed no emotion. One eye was damaged, and he was disfigured down that side of his face. The top of his head was bald with shaved hair round the sides and an unkempt beard. As he walked towards Rhys I could see the armband of the Federation. It was a blue globe with a dagger through it; underneath were the words 'A Free People'.

The guard dragged Rhys over to the commanding officer.

'On the ground, vermin!' the guard snarled as he violently yanked the noose forward, causing Rhys to fall at the feet of the captain.

The captain walked over, raised one of his big black Federation-issue military boots and stamped on the side of Rhys's face; with a dull thud, Rhys fell to the ground. The captain kept his boot on his head, pressing his face into the mud. Rhys's arms flailed wildly as he struggled for breath.

My heart was beating fast. I wanted to do something, but there was nothing I could do. My eyes welled up as I watched the way they treated us like animals.

Then I saw the captain reach for his weapon. It was a long black wooden club. As he pulled it from the holster on the side of his trousers he seemed to twist it. This must have activated it, as two long needles protruded from the end of the device, each one about five inches long. Then he pressed another area of the weapon and I heard it start to buzz as two bolts of electricity sparked from between the needles. I had heard stories about these execution sticks, but I had assumed they were just rumours.

He raised the device, but before plunging it down he stopped and looked at the people.

Rhys was too weary to struggle now, and could only squirm under the pressure of the boot on the side of his face. His face was being pressed into a puddle of muddy water and he was gasping for air.

'This is the price of your stupid beliefs,' the captain shouted to the frightened group of people cowering before him. 'They will not be tolerated!'

Then he plunged the needles deep into Rhys's neck. His limbs flailed around violently and uncontrollably as the current passed through his body. His screams soon died out, and he was left twitching on the cold forest floor.

My legs went weak at the sight of it all and I buckled under my own weight. I couldn't stand; I was only supported by the two walls I was trapped between.

Then the captain pulled out the stick. He didn't even look down at Rhys, knowing that he was dead. He walked menacingly over to those who were being prepared for transport.

'Any of you put one foot out of line, and . . .' He turned and gestured towards Rhys's lifeless body as it lay in the mud.

He walked back over to the young guard who was still standing near me.

'Pack them up for transport, search the house and then we continue the hunt.'

'Yes, sir,' replied the guard. His voice was not as confident as before; he seemed scared. The captain could sense his fear and walked right over to him, looked him in the eye and said, 'Do you understand, soldier?'

The young guard composed himself and more confidently replied, 'Yes, sir,' raising his clenched fist to his chest, a salute I had seen the guards give to each other before.

I could see the others being shackled for transport back to the intern camps. From what I had heard of these camps, they were little better than death.

The young guard, following his captain's command, turned and walked towards the house. If they found me or my sisters, we would surely be killed. I just prayed that my sisters would not cough or make a noise. I could hear him walking from room to room, the floorboards creaking with the weight of his footsteps. I heard him approach the doorway of the room where I was hiding. I held my breath and froze.

The guard walked around the room kicking over piles of rubbish with his boot and opening the cupboard doors. He turned towards the wall and kicked an old can from the floor. As it hit the wall where I was hiding, the noise startled me, and I let out a small yelp.

He heard me, and turned towards the wall. He just stared at the wall; it was almost as if he didn't want to find anyone. Eventually, he slowly walked over to where I was and bent down towards the cracks in the wall. I couldn't move in order to escape his view; he came right up to the wall, pressing his face against the wood. His eyes peered through the crack directly into mine. We just stared at each other. Then he turned and straightened himself up.

He stood with his back to the wall for a moment, then suddenly turned back and punched his clenched fist into the wall. The old dry timber was easy to break. I lurched to one side as much as I could to avoid being hit full on. As his hand came through the wall he scrambled around trying to feel for me. He pulled away some more wall panels and managed to get hold of my hair. He tugged violently at it, dragging my face through the hole he had made. The broken timbers were pressing deep into my cheeks, drawing blood, as he pulled my head through.

Then something changed. Seeing my exposed face, terrified, bleeding and with tears in my eyes, he seemed to recognize me.

'Chloe,' he whispered under his breath. 'No—what are you . . .' Unable to finish his thought, he became visibly distressed.

As I composed myself I was able to look at him properly. I knew this man; we were in the same class together at school.

As he stared at me, I could see him processing his memories. We now had a human connection and it was burning his conscience. All he had been taught was telling him we were animals and had no right to life. But now, confronted with his emotions and the stark reality, he knew that was a lie.

'Please, leave us,' I pleaded with him.

He let go of my hair and stepped back. He looked at his own hands as if in disbelief at what he had done. His eyes were now welling up with tears.

'Leave through the back of the house and run as far and as fast as you can,' he said.

With that, he turned and left the house. I never saw him again.

I crept out of the wall and across into the next room. I opened the trapdoor to the basement where my sisters were still hiding and pulled them out. We exited the house at the back and began to run into the forest.

We didn't say a word; we just ran as far as we could until we couldn't take another step, then collapsed onto the ground.

After a few minutes we heard the sound of steps nearby. Thinking the guards had caught us, we sat up to look. Two people stood in front of us, but they were not Federation soldiers.

'Who are you?' I asked.

One of the two, the smaller one, stepped forward. Clearly not wanting to intimidate me, she lowered her weapon and knelt to our level.

'Chloe, it's OK, it's me.'

I wiped the dirt and blood from my face to see who it was talking to us. As I focused on the figure before me, I saw that it was Talia. She had left our camp months before to serve in the resistance army, but we never knew if she had made it or not.

'Talia,' I said almost in unbelief.

'It's me, Chloe; I'm serving with the resistance army.'

When I heard this statement, the emotion of the last

twenty-four hours overwhelmed me, and I began to sob uncontrollably.

The other soldier then stepped forward. He was older and looked battle-hardened. Putting his hand on Talia's shoulder, he whispered to her, 'We need to leave, now.'

He then turned to us and said, 'You're safe. We can take you to a city of refuge.'

FACT OR FICTION?

Although the above story is clearly a fictional narrative, the main elements from the story have been drawn from real-world ideologies and carried to their logical conclusions. Many times, history has shown us the consequences of what happens when human life is devalued. In the previous chapter, we looked at some of the results of a human life being reduced to nothing more than that of an animal in the evolutionary process.

In this chapter, we will examine a concept that is held dear by many people today, both religious and non-religious: that is, the concept of human equality, the idea that men and women, young and old, are equal in value and should be given the same rights. Most people today would be aghast if you implied that they did not believe in this concept. 'How dare you!' they would say. Yet for those who still cherish this 'ideal' and believe it is something that must be maintained, what is the ground for this belief? Does their worldview—their understanding of reality and the framework of beliefs upon which they build their lives—provide them with a basis for holding a view which affords equality to all people?

What we actually find today is that many people who

affirm this belief in the equality of persons also subscribe to other beliefs that completely undermine it. The belief that all people are equal is actually an enduring legacy of the Judaeo-Christian worldview, the specific belief that men and women were created in the image of God. From this we derive our understanding of and basis for human rights and ethics. If there is no justification for believing in the equality of persons, or that humans have equal value, what is to stop us treating each other in a way that represents this? It was not commonly accepted in the ancient world, and what we are witnessing today in the West is the undermining of this belief as we jettison our biblical heritage in favour of a naturalistic understanding of humanity.

WHERE DOES EQUALITY BEGIN?

It was the atheist Friedrich Nietzsche who said, 'Another Christian concept, no less crazy: the concept of equality of souls before God. This concept furnishes the prototype of all theories of equal rights.'[1] Was he right? Of course, those who refuse to believe that humans are a special creation of God have two choices: invent some other way to justify the belief in human equality, or else (the only alternative) accept that human equality is a myth. Most take the first option, and they talk about the progress of society being responsible for our belief in equal rights. They will point to myriads of examples of secular laws and morals that have been put in place without any reference to God. But this is missing the point. The issue is not whether humanity can collectively make ethical and moral laws with reference to the equality of human persons, but how these laws are justified and grounded from within the secular worldview.

The issue boils down to this: are humans merely animals, or are we special creations? Is it naturalism or theism that best explains what it means to be human? And which one provides a better foundation for human rights? A graphic story is often told about Joseph Stalin, the Soviet leader who was responsible for so much death and devastation among his own people (usually reckoned to be around 20 million people). Soviet novelist Chingiz Aitmatov told the following story, which has been paraphrased here by Ravi Zacharias:

> On one occasion, so it was narrated, Stalin called for a live chicken and proceeded to use it to make an unforgettable point before some of his henchmen. Forcefully clutching the chicken in one hand, with the other he began to systematically pluck out its feathers. As the chicken struggled in vain to escape, he continued with the painful denuding until the bird was completely stripped. 'Now you watch,' Stalin said as he placed the chicken on the floor and walked away with some bread crumbs in his hand. Incredibly, the fear-crazed chicken hobbled toward him and clung to the legs of his trousers. Stalin threw a handful of grain to the bird, and it began to follow him around the room. He turned to his dumbfounded colleagues and said quietly, 'This is the way to rule the people. Did you see how that chicken followed me for food, even though I had caused it such torture? People are like that chicken. If you inflict inordinate pain on them they will follow you for food the rest of their lives.'[2]

Are people really like that chicken? Or are we just like another form of animal? Stalin was consistent in his belief and carried it to its logical conclusion. Yes, but we have learnt the lessons of history, haven't we? Tragically, I don't believe we have.

The Nobel Prize-winning Russian novelist and outspoken critic of the Soviet Union Aleksandr Solzhenitsyn delivered the Templeton Lecture in 1983, in which he said the following words:

More than half a century ago, while I was still a child, I recall hearing a number of older people offer the following explanation for the great disasters that had befallen Russia: *Men have forgotten God; that's why all this has happened.*

Since then I have spent well-nigh fifty years working on the history of our Revolution; in the process I have read hundreds of books, collected hundreds of personal testimonies, and have already contributed eight volumes of my own toward the effort of clearing away the rubble left by that upheaval. But if I were asked today to formulate as concisely as possible the main cause of the ruinous Revolution that swallowed up some sixty million of our people, I could not put it more accurately than to repeat: *Men have forgotten God; that's why all this has happened.*[3]

A VANISHING LEGACY

As we survey the landscape of Western nations today, it seems we are doing everything in our power to make this same mistake. Talk of God is considered passé. Christianity is often reduced to ridiculous stereotypes and soundbites that have no real meaning or connection to the world. The media displays a flagrant disregard for Christian ethics, denigrating it wherever possible. The education system is intent on pushing a hard-line, naturalistic account of origins to entire generations, and popular atheist writings that rant about all things concerning God are gobbled up by a wanting public.

We are walking precariously upon the edge of a precipice which threatens to destroy our very foundations.

Solzhenitsyn continued:

> The 1920's in the USSR witnessed an uninterrupted procession of victims and martyrs amongst the Orthodox clergy . . . Tens of thousands of priests, monks and nuns, pressured by the Chekists to renounce the Word of God, were tortured, shot in cellars, sent to camps, exiled to the desolate tundra of the far North, or turned out into the streets in their old age without food or shelter. All these Christian martyrs went unswervingly to their deaths for the faith; instances of apostasy were few and far between. For tens of millions of laymen access to the Church was blocked, and they were forbidden to bring up their children in the Faith: religious parents were wrenched from their children and thrown into prison, while the children were turned from the faith by threats and lies . . .[4]

Is this attitude towards religion so far removed from the fictional elements of the story related earlier? And can we not hear the echoes of this in the words of modern atheists, like Richard Dawkins, who has called religion a 'virus of the mind' and said that parents bringing up their children with these beliefs are guilty of 'child abuse'?[5] Richard Dawkins even uses language such as 'infecting the next generation': 'for many people, part of growing up is killing off the virus of faith with a good strong dose of rational thinking. But if an individual doesn't succeed in shaking it off, his mind is stuck in a permanent state of infancy, and there is a real danger that he will infect the next generation.'[6]

The unspoken question arising from such inflammatory statements is this: how do we stop them infecting the next generation? We could ban them from speaking in public, remove all religion from the education curriculum, ridicule it in popular media, distort what it teaches, ban the wearing of any outward symbols, force them out of jobs. It all sounds very familiar, doesn't it? If this doesn't work, maybe we could close down their places of worship, or even burn them down. And ultimately, if these things do not work, the only way to stop this malignant infection spreading is to . . . (well, I refer you back to the story above). Of course, in reality, Dawkins' statements are nothing more than emotionally charged rhetoric with no evidential support. They are really little more than his personal opinion, contributing nothing to disprove the rationality of belief in God or to prove the hypothesis of atheism.

LISTEN TO THE EXPERTS

Most people in the Western world today go about their lives with the understanding that it is right to treat people equally with respect and dignity—or at least, they profess to believe that. For the most part, people want to see other human beings treated respectfully and without undue discrimination. However, ask someone why they believe this, and you begin to see the position unravel. 'It's the right thing to do,' someone might say. 'But right according to whom?' we might ask back. This view assumes that there is such a thing as 'right' and 'wrong', but where do we get these concepts? 'Because we're all brothers, it's the human thing to do,' another might respond; but what is a human, and who are you to say what is and isn't the 'human' thing to do? What is your authority for that?

Please do not misunderstand me: I am glad that people

do believe this, and I will demonstrate why they do so a little later, but the point I am raising is that these beliefs need to be grounded in order to be rationally justifiable and objective, or else they simply end up reflecting the subjective opinion of man.

If you were to probe the beliefs of these same people a little more, you would probably discover that most of them also subscribe to the Darwinian account of human history. We evolved from higher primates; trace the chain of evolution far back enough down the tree and we arrive at the 'primordial soup'! Man is part of the animal kingdom. If this is true, it is hard to find defensible reasons why humans are intrinsically more valuable than other creatures. Darwin commented, 'Man in his arrogance thinks himself a great work, worthy of the interposition of a deity. More humble, and I believe truer, to consider him created from animals.'[7]

The prevalence of the Darwinian worldview has continued to erode the lingering belief that humans are somehow special in the universe. Palaeontologist Stephen J. Gould stated that 'biology has shifted our status from a simulacrum of God to a naked, upright ape'.[8] Princeton ethicist Peter Singer often bemoans the special status that man is afforded in the universe, as his book *Unsanctifying Human Life* makes abundantly clear. He has said:

> All we are doing is catching up with Darwin. He showed in the 19th century that we are simply animals. Humans had imagined we were a separate part of Creation, that there was some magical line between Us and Them. Darwin's theory undermined the foundations of that entire Western way of thinking about the place of our species in the universe.[9]

Such a radical undermining of the Judaeo-Christian worldview, and the place it affords to humanity, means that all basis for ethics and morals is also undermined. Harvard biologist E. O. Wilson states that 'ethics as we understand it is an illusion fobbed off on us by our genes to get us to co-operate'.[10] In a similar vein, evolutionist William Provine has written that 'modern science [i.e. evolution] directly implies that there are no inherent moral or ethical laws, no absolute guiding principles for human society'.[11]

It was Nietzsche who popularized the 'God is dead' movement in the nineteenth century. He also predicted that the next two centuries would be the bloodiest centuries in all history. He understood that God was the source of our morality and that removing God would be equal to removing the foundation for morality and ethics. In his world, God was no longer the source of values, so man would now decide his own values. The problem is that, in this view, man is descended from the animal kingdom, and therefore is most likely to embrace the values we so often see in the animal world—the survival of the fittest, or, as Nietzsche put it, the '*libido dominandi*' (the lust to dominate). Morality is no longer given to us by divine revelation but decided upon by ourselves. One only has to look back a few years in history to witness the devastation that such a view has perpetrated upon humanity. Nietzsche's prophecy was correct: the last two centuries have been the bloodiest in all of human history, with over 130 million human deaths attributed to atheistic regimes.

MODERN FRUIT AND A DISAPPEARING ROOT

Such tragic events in the history of mankind clearly illustrate the way our view of human equality manifests itself in culture, for good or for evil. Views that place humans at the end of an evolutionary chain will produce fruit in keeping with that belief. How tragic it is that the formerly rich Judaeo-Christian foundations of the Western world, which historically placed great value on human life, are being undermined by a rabid secularism that removes the only objective source of human equality: that all humans are image-bearers of God. If the trunk of the tree is chopped down, how much longer will the fruit on the branches survive? As Margaret Thatcher said in a speech to the Church of Scotland: 'I think back to many discussions in my early life when we all agreed that if you try to take the fruits of Christianity without its roots, the fruits will wither. And they will not come again unless you nurture the roots.'[12]

As our culture continues to try to expunge every trace of our heritage, the result will be that the value placed on human life is lost. We continue down this road to the detriment of our society. Our culture's trajectory will only change when it begins to nurture the root which supports human rights and Christian values.

THE IMAGE OF GOD

So what is it that separates us from the animal kingdom in a unique way? Why is human life so precious to God? To understand this, we need to consult the Manufacturer's instructions. This means that we must understand the 'teleology', or design, of mankind. In the first chapter of the Bible we find these words:

> Then God said, 'Let us make man in our image, after our likeness. And let them have dominion over the fish of the sea and over the

birds of the heavens and over the livestock and over all the earth and over every creeping thing that creeps on the earth.

So God created man in his own image,
in the image of God he created him;
male and female he created them.

(Genesis 1:26–27)

The Bible clearly teaches here that human beings are created in the image of God. This distinct honour is not afforded to anything else in the creation narrative. It is the sole privilege of mankind, bestowed on us by our loving Creator. This implies that we are made to be like God in some fundamental and profound ways.

The interesting thing we need to grasp about an image is that it cannot exist by itself: it only finds its explanation in the original which it is imaging. This profoundly impacts our question of who we are. It means that if we really want to understand what it is to be human, we must first understand something about who God is—the source of the image. It also means that our true identity is not contingent upon how beautiful or successful we are; rather, it is totally dependent upon Him. Any search for understanding must begin with this. The Reformer John Calvin said it this way: 'No man can survey himself without forthwith turning his thoughts towards the God in whom he lives and moves; because it is perfectly obvious, that the endowments which we possess cannot be from ourselves.'[13]

So what are these particular endowments that point beyond ourselves? What does it mean to be made in the image of God? Although theologians have discussed this question for a long time, and the debate still rages, there are a number of truths that stand out as ways in which we resemble God. Perhaps the most profound truth, the thing that sets us apart as unique, is that we are spiritual beings. This is one way in which we 'image God', because God is spirit (John 4:24). Part of our uniqueness is that man consists of two distinct parts: a body and a soul.[14] Genesis 2:7 says that 'the LORD God formed man of the dust of the ground, and breathed into his nostrils the breath of life; and man became a living soul' (KJV). The soul seems to be responsible for the areas of humanity that relate to the spiritual elements of ourselves, such as our individual subjective consciousness, self-awareness, emotions, moral awareness, rationality, cognition and the ability to make free choices. The soul is an invisible entity that is distinct from the physical body. Although the human brain does play a part in experiencing many of these things, it is nonetheless the soul which originates them and interacts with the brain.

Providing a satisfactory definition of the soul is difficult because it is a non-physical entity, yet the Bible provides some insights into the dual nature of man. The Bible commands us to love God with the heart, soul and strength (Luke 10:27). Elsewhere, Paul argues that the conscience of a man can convict him of the moral law of God (Romans 2:15). Paul seems to affirm the dualistic nature of man when he argues that to 'be away from the body' is to be 'at home with the Lord' (2 Corinthians 5:7–8). Jesus also clearly affirms man's dualistic nature on many occasions in the Scriptures. A clear example is where He says to His disciples, 'do not fear those who kill the body but cannot kill the soul. Rather fear him who can destroy both soul and body in hell' (Matthew 10:28). As the philosopher Paul Copan affirms, 'The scriptures strongly favour the view that there is an immaterial aspect to human beings—the soul, mind or spirit—which is potentially separable from the material body—even though it is not the final state.'[15]

Of course, within a strictly materialist view, man is nothing more than the sum of his physical parts and there is no room for immaterial entities such as the soul. The soul is declared to be fiction. As atheist philosopher Daniel Dennett has said, 'the idea of immaterial souls . . . has outlived its credibility thanks to the advances of the natural sciences'.[16] This view, sometimes known as physicalism, argues that these human elements are nothing but the result of chemical reactions in the brain, simply the result of completely natural processes taking place. Those who hold to physicalism have obviously presupposed a naturalistic worldview which denies that anything exists outside of the physical realm, and thus physicalism must be true and dualism must be rejected.

So which of these two views of the nature of man can better account for these unique human endowments? Is dualism or physicalism a better explanation for consciousness and free will? As we will briefly argue, biblical anthropology, with its dualistic understanding of man, can provide a much better account of human endowments such as consciousness and free will than can a naturalistic anthropology. In fact, these two particular endowments have proven to be quite a puzzle for materialistic philosophers to explain. This issue is often referred to as the mind/body problem in philosophical circles.

THE MYSTERY OF CONSCIOUSNESS

Consciousness remains one of the most elusive aspects of a

materialistic anthropology to explain. To simply deny it is very hard, as that goes against all our natural intuition. As philosopher Keith Ward explains, 'materialism is immensely counter intuitive. It conflicts with our common-sense view that all human knowledge begins from personal experience, that we have thoughts and feelings that no one else can experience, that we are free to plan the future, and that our intentions make a real difference to the world. In short, materialism has a real problem with consciousness.'[17]

The other option is to try to explain it away, but this proves difficult as all the materialist has in his explanatory toolkit are physical descriptions of reality. And these seem to fall short of the needed scope to account for things that are clearly unique attributes of the mental life. There is a difference between mind and matter, a difference in kind between mental states and physical states. The two cannot be identical; they are different things. The basic intuition that arises from a person's self-perception, or subjective first-person identity, is that it is not really plausible to attribute the broad range of emotions and the free expression of rationality simply to the results of synaptic firings—that is, chemical signalling between neurons in the brain. Yet this is exactly what physicalism must do in order to survive. Joseph LeDoux's popular-level book *Synaptic Self: How Our Brains Become Who We Are* concludes with these words: 'You are your synapses. They are who you are.'[18] This becomes the ultimate physicalist creed.

Yet does such a reductionist account really explain the concept of 'self'? To say that all our self-understanding, private thoughts and personal emotions are just physical reactions, entirely physical processes occurring within the brain, is not actually an explanation of consciousness; it is just a statement *about* consciousness, one that actually raises more questions than it solves. If the universe is the result of a completely mechanistic unconscious process, and if everything in it is made up of unconscious physical particles, then by itself it cannot suddenly bring consciousness into the equation. Mind and matter are two very different things. To explain away or deny the life of the mind is counter-intuitive. The burden of proof must be shouldered by those who claim otherwise. Yet, for those who maybe wish otherwise, the problem remains. This was exemplified very clearly by philosopher Thomas Nagel, who, although an atheist, wrote a book against the modern materialist approach and its failure to account for something as integral as the mind. He argued:

> Consciousness is the most conspicuous obstacle to a comprehensive naturalism that relies only on the resources of physical science. The existence of consciousness seems to imply that the physical description of the universe, in spite of its richness and explanatory power, is only part of the truth, and that the natural order is far less austere than it would be if physics and chemistry accounted for everything. If we take this problem seriously, and follow out its implications, it threatens to unravel the entire naturalistic world picture.[19]

He is right: the threat is real. Yet to concede what Nagel has done is more than most materialists are willing to do. Therefore, the only option left is to claim ignorance and hope that, one day, advances in neuroscience will solve the problem. But for now, most must agree with Jerry Fodor and admit that 'nobody has the slightest idea how anything material could be conscious'.[20] This is known as 'The Hard Problem' of consciousness. The problem is put rather ironically by atheist Colin McGinn: 'How did evolution convert the water of biological tissue into the wine of consciousness?'[21]

THE BIBLICAL EXPLANATION

While this may pose a problem for the materialist's understanding of man, the same is not true for the biblical concept of man. More than that, the entire theistic worldview is supported by the fact of consciousness. If we follow the sequence logically we arrive at a theistic conclusion. Minds or consciousness are a brute fact of the living world and, as already stated, physicalism cannot provide a basis for this. The best explanation for the dualistic nature of human beings is that the existence of independent minds actually stems from an original infinite mind. This is the biblical teaching. As it has often been pointed out, you either start with particles or you start with a mind. The Bible states that 'In the beginning was the Word [*logos*],' which means the divine mind (John 1:1).[22] This mind cannot be natural, so it must be supernatural; this mind had a plan and design in creating, so it must be a personal mind; it cannot be one mind in a long chain of minds, in order to avoid infinite regress, so it must be a necessary uncaused mind; it is not a mind that somehow emerged from matter, but is an eternal self-existent mind; it cannot be part of the physical universe, so it must transcend space and time and be immaterial; and, finally, this mind must be powerful enough to create all matter and energy that compose the physical universe.

All these features provide an apt description of the God (the ultimate Mind) revealed to us in the Bible. God is the eternal self-existent being, 'I AM WHO I AM' (Exodus 3:14), who is responsible for creating both the material and the immaterial world. Out of all the beautiful and magnificent creatures that He spoke into existence, there was only one that He chose to fashion in such a way that they would have the honour of bearing His image. Mankind would consist of both physical and spiritual components, which would be designed in the foreknowledge of God to interact in the very way He purposed. The theistic worldview, and in particular the Christian worldview, provides a wonderful foundation for the sort of complexity we see between consciousness and brain states in our everyday experience. As King David cried out in the Psalms:

For you formed my inward parts;
  you knitted me together in my mother's womb.
I praise you, for I am fearfully and wonderfully made.
Wonderful are your works;
  my soul knows it very well.
My frame was not hidden from you,
when I was being made in secret,
  intricately woven in the depths of the earth.
Your eyes saw my unformed substance;
in your book were written, every one of them,
  the days that were formed for me,
  when as yet there was none of them.

(Psalm 139:13–16)

MAN AS A MORAL BEING

The well-known Christmas song 'Santa Claus Is Coming to Town' includes these words:

He's making a list,
And checking it twice;
He's gonna find out who's naughty and nice
Santa Claus is coming to town

He sees you when you're sleeping
And he knows when you're awake
He knows when you've been bad or good
So be good for goodness' sake!

Naughty or nice, bad or good: where do these concepts come from? The very acknowledgement of good or bad behaviour, which we see in so many ways throughout the world, is testament to another aspect of man that owes its origin to the image of God. This is the moral awareness that is intrinsic and ultimately unique to humanity. Humans are not only spiritual beings but also moral beings. The apostle Paul, in the book of Romans, talks about this moral conscience that is given to mankind. He writes, 'For when Gentiles, who do not have the law, by nature do what the law requires, they are a law to themselves, even though they do not have the law. They show that the work of the law is written on their hearts, while their conscience also bears witness, and their conflicting thoughts accuse or even excuse them' (Romans 2:14–15). This explains why humans have this inherent concept of right and wrong.

To be sure, this does not imply that people will always adhere to this standard; quite the opposite, in fact, as will be explained in the following chapter. This teaching also answers the common atheist objection that atheists can live perfectly good lives without needing to believe in God. They argue that God is not needed for moral values. Actually, this objection simply proves the Christian viewpoint but also misunderstands the argument. Firstly, the verse we read in Romans applies to all people, regardless of their particular religious beliefs—atheist or theist. All people are made in the image of God, with the law of God written upon their hearts, so we should not be at all surprised to see people who do not happen to believe in God participating in moral activities. Secondly, and most importantly, we are not even arguing that people cannot be moral without belief in God; this is beside the point. The claim we are making is that there is no way to ground the existence of morality itself in a completely material universe.

THE MORAL ARGUMENT

The philosopher Immanuel Kant wrote in his famous treatise *Critique of Practical Reason*, 'Two things fill the mind with ever new and increasing admiration and reverence . . . the starry heavens above me and the moral law within me.'[23] The existence of a moral law has been used by many to argue for the existence of a moral law-giver. Most famously in contemporary literature is the moral argument formulated by C. S. Lewis in his book *Mere Christianity*. Lewis carefully crafts his argument around three main premises. Regarding the existence of a moral law, Lewis comments that 'human beings, all over the earth, have this curious idea that they ought to behave in a certain way, and cannot really get rid of it'.[24] Of course, we all believe that certain moral standards are to be preferred over others, but, as Lewis comments, 'the moment you say that one set of ideas can be better than another, you are, in fact, measuring them both by a standard'.[25] From this, Lewis argues that if the moral law is real, and it is not a physical law, this implies there must be a moral law-giver. And, thirdly, he points out that this moral law-giver must be transcendent, or an entity beyond the physical universe: this 'must be something beyond the actual facts of human behaviour'.

Christian philosopher Ravi Zacharias, a great admirer of Lewis, phrases the argument this way: 'When you say there is evil, aren't you admitting there is good? When you accept the existence of goodness, you must affirm a moral law on the basis of which to differentiate between good and evil. But when you admit to a moral law, you must posit a moral lawgiver.'[26]

Yet simply proving a moral law-giver is only half the battle. As Lewis points out, 'I am not yet within a hundred miles of the God of Christian theology.'[27] Still, the God of Christian theology is a much better explanation for the existence of a moral law that is beyond the physical universe than any of the alternatives; it seems more rational to believe that a specific set of laws originated from a mind who is intensely concerned with right conduct. The conclusion that Lewis draws is this: if we do in fact live in a moral universe with a mind behind it, one that is the source of this law, we have reason to be uneasy. For 'there is nothing indulgent about the moral law. It is hard as nails. It tells you to do the straight thing and it does not seem to care how painful, or dangerous, or difficult it is to do.'[28] The truth, as we all know, is that we often fail to live up to this law. This means that if 'there does exist an absolute goodness it must hate most of what we do. This is the terrible fix we are in.'[29] This is what Christian theology classes as the bad news that must be explained before the gospel becomes 'good news'. In this vein, Lewis masterfully takes the argument further to argue for the Christian God: 'It is after you have realized that there is a Moral law, and a Power behind the law, and that you have broken that law and put yourself wrong with that Power—it is after all this, and not a moment sooner, that Christianity begins to talk.'[30]

The beautiful message of the Christian gospel must begin with this tragedy: a tragedy that is pivotal to understanding part of who we are as human beings, where we stand in the bigger picture and what God has in store for us.

WHAT CAN NATURALISM OFFER?

Consistent naturalists, if they are being totally honest with themselves, must admit that there can be no such thing as an objective 'right' and 'wrong' within their worldview, no specific standard that exists independent of mankind. President of the American Atheists David Silverman put it this way: 'There is no objective moral standard. We are responsible for our own actions.'[31]

If there is any sense of moral obligation, it has either been decided upon collectively by the community—and does not necessarily hold any binding imperative upon another community who may feel differently—or, as atheist philosopher Michael Ruse has said, all 'ethics as we understand it is an illusion fobbed off on us by our genes to get us to co-operate . . . ethics is a shared illusion of the human race'.[32] Yet is the concept of an 'illusion' really an adequate explanation to account for life's experiences? If someone was to break into your house, destroy your personal belongings, murder your spouse and leave you battered and bruised, you would undoubtedly feel that you had been wronged. You would call the police! But imagine if the policeman who arrived at your house said, 'Sorry, sir. While I agree this is a most unpleasant experience you have been through, I don't think anyone has actually done anything morally wrong. What you're feeling is an illusion, a trick being played on you by your genes. Have a good day'—you would feel a strong sense of injustice! When your belief system forces you to live with such contradictions, it is a sign that there is a problem with it—it cannot account for all of reality, the very thing it is supposed to do.

Many atheists display this sort of tension in their lives as they try to live with these contradictions. Richard Dawkins is a very clear example of this. He writes, 'The universe we observe has precisely the properties we should expect if there is, at the bottom, no design, no purpose, no evil and no good. Nothing but blind, pitiless, indifference. DNA neither knows nor cares. DNA just is. And we dance to its music.'[33] This is a beautifully crafted explanation of the materialist reality. The problem, though, is that it can't be consistently believed. If there is no good and no evil, it seems more than a little disingenuous for Dawkins himself to have written a whole book (*The God Delusion*) in which all he does is raise supposed moral complaints about God and those who follow

Him. Elsewhere, Dawkins admits that he does not wish to live according to his Darwinian principles, saying, 'As a scientist I am a passionate Darwinian,' but at the same time, 'I am a passionate anti-Darwinian when it comes to politics and how we should conduct our human affairs.'[34]

The expression 'have your cake and eat it' seems appropriate here. Basically, many atheists want to borrow capital from the Christian worldview when it comes to ethics, but not acknowledge that this is what they are doing. The implications of being entirely consistent with their own worldview are too severe. However, there are some who are willing to be consistent with their atheism. Nietzsche often complained about the way his contemporaries failed to grasp that, now 'God is dead', everything that is built upon the Christian worldview must go too. For Nietzsche, that very definitely included Christian morality, which had shaped much of the Western world. He said in his *Twilight of the Idols*:

When one gives up Christian belief one thereby deprives oneself of the right to Christian morality. For the latter is absolutely not self-evident . . . Christianity is a system, a consistently thought-out and complete view of things. If one breaks out of it a fundamental idea, the belief in God, one thereby breaks the whole thing to pieces . . . it stands or falls with the belief in God.[35]

The problem is, if concepts such as right and wrong do not exist, it is very hard to condemn someone else's behaviour, no matter how evil it may be. At most we can express our personal opinion about it, but we cannot condemn it as being morally wrong. Nietzsche's point that it is unacceptable to borrow moral categories from the Christian worldview in order to appease our conscience on these issues is absolutely correct. However, the logical conclusions from this are unsettling—which is why most people are happy to ignore the implications and continue holding onto an inconsistent worldview.

NUREMBURG AND NATURAL LAW

There have been times in history when the strength of the moral law has been brought to the forefront of the public's conscience and used to condemn abhorrent acts of evil. The Holocaust still stands out as one of the most heinous acts of evil in modern history: the systematic slaughter of over 6 million Jews, 1.1 million of whom were children, and of over 5 million people of various other minorities is testament to the existence of evil in this world. It is not only the fact of so much death, but the callous and systematic manner in which so many lost their lives, whether at the hands of doctors conducting warped medical experiments, in the ovens or under the poisonous gas showers. With the Nazis' defeat in the Second World War by the Allied forces, the true depravity of their regime was exposed to the world. Such was the horror of the Holocaust that the Nazis were tried in 1946 for war crimes at the Nuremberg Trials in Germany.

The trial itself raises some interesting questions for us today. The defence attorney for the Nazis argued that they were simply obeying the orders of Hitler, which at the time had the force of law in the German state. Obedience to the law of the land, he claimed, could not be the basis for criminal trial. He further argued that no internationally recognized standard by which states could judge one another's aims existed at the time. Therefore, threatening to prosecute the Nazis for perpetrating acts that, at the time, did not carry any punishment (and were actually sanctioned by state law) was invalid. What right did America, Britain or any other nation have to hold the Nazis to account for their actions? What law code was being used? Invoking law codes from another nation—for example, British law—in order to try a people who were German and who had their own law would pose huge problems legally. So on what legal basis were the Nazis being condemned? What law had they broken? None at the time. Does this somehow lessen the evil of their actions? No. But for those who hold to a worldview that rejects the concept of objective right and wrong, it poses a serious problem: on what basis do you condemn the Nazis? They broke no international law at the time.

The response of the prosecution highlighted this issue. Robert Jackson, US Supreme Court Justice and Chief Prosecutor at Nuremberg, opened with these remarks: 'The Charter of this Tribunal evidences a faith that the law is not only to govern the conduct of little men, but that even rulers are, as Lord Chief Justice Coke [said] to King James, "under God and the law".'[36] He was clearly suggesting that there exists a higher standard by which to judge. The Chief Prosecutor for the United Kingdom was even clearer: 'Ultimately the rights of men, made as all men are made in the image of God, are fundamental.'[37]

A HIGHER LAW

Finally, in his closing remarks, Justice Jackson seemed to

place the final authority for the entire tribunal on a law that transcends the human laws of nations: 'As an International Military Tribunal, it rises above the provincial and transient, and seeks guidance not only from International Law but also from the basic principles of jurisprudence, which are assumptions of civilisation and which long have found embodiment in the codes of all nations.'[38] The only law that rises above the 'provincial and transient' (of place and time) is the law of God, or the moral law. How interesting it is that, when confronted with what could only reasonably be described as pure evil, the moral law of God had to be invoked in order to condemn.

This raises some uncomfortable questions for us today. In a culture that has become increasingly secularized, and in which appeals to cosmic authority in relation to legal disputes are usually met with ridicule, would we be able to prosecute the Nazis today based on that same standard? This is a sobering question; the evisceration of God from our society leaves us in a moral 'no man's land', and such a question should cause us to stop and think about the rampant moral relativism that currently strangles our culture. The mantra that has been consistently shoved down the throats of our young people in educational institutions is that relativism is the correct attitude to adopt, the tolerant option. To sustain this relativism, one must first deny the objective nature of truth itself. But without truth, all standards disappear, and people become the sole arbiters of their individual little 'truths'. Whatever we decide is true becomes true for us.

Is it any wonder that, in 2016, Oxford Dictionaries declared 'post-truth' to be its international word of the year? It defined it as an adjective 'relating to or denoting circumstances in which objective facts are less influential in shaping public opinion than appeals to emotion and personal belief'.[39] This does seem to provide a very good description of our culture today—one where 'facts' are determined by emotionally charged rhetoric and personal opinions. To disagree with someone's opinion is considered intolerant, and dissenting from this post-truth mindset is seen as the height of bigotry. To protect against this, many educational institutions provide their fragile students with 'safe spaces', where they can avoid such intrusions into their fantasy reality, and also 'trigger warnings', to prepare them for the fact that they are about to hear something they do not agree with. It would be laughable if it was not true.

Such an infantile approach to truth will result in a generation with no foundations and no standards for anything except their own immature feelings. This in turn will contribute to them having underdeveloped and insecure identities. A nation that is asked to make laws based upon such a worldview will be a fractured and divided nation, unable to live with the inconsistencies its own ideology has created. What is the antidote to such thinking? It is not to exalt human reason as the only source able to discover truth, as the Enlightenment thinkers did, nor is it to reject all concepts of truth and rely solely on emotions, as our culture does today. Instead, we need to return to the concept of revelation, revealed truth. Truth is not determined by our subjective standards but is revealed by the very source of truth: God Himself. Jesus declared Himself not simply to know truth, but actually to be truth. Truth is an attribute of God: 'Jesus said to him, "I am the way, and the truth, and the life. No one comes to the Father except through me"' (John 14:6).

ARE YOU FREE TO KEEP READING?

Perhaps one of the best speeches in cinematic history (in my opinion) is made in the movie *Braveheart*. The famous speech given by warrior leader William Wallace (Mel Gibson) to his band of Scottish rebels, as they prepare to fight the vast forces of the English army at the Battle of Stirling, is designed to instil courage:

WILLIAM WALLACE: I am William Wallace! And I see a whole army of my countrymen, here in defiance of tyranny. You've come to fight as free men . . . and free men you are. What will you do with that freedom? Will you fight?

SOLDIER: Fight? Against that? No! We will run. And we will live.

WILLIAM WALLACE: Aye, fight and you may die. Run, and you'll live . . . at least a while. And dying in your beds, many years from now, would you be willin' to trade ALL the days, from this day to that, for one chance, just one chance, to come back here and tell our enemies that they may take our lives, but they'll never take . . . OUR FREEDOM![40]

Many armies have marched, and many soldiers have spilt their blood upon battlefields, in search of freedom. The aim of such wars is usually to seek freedom from the reign of tyrannical governments or leaders. These freedoms are worth fighting for. There are other freedoms we cherish and consider essential to a free society. The freedom of speech, the freedom of conscience and the freedom of religion are three of the main elements most people expect in a free society. Yet there is one more type of freedom that is even more fundamental than all these: the freedom of the will. Do you really have the ability to freely choose? Or are your actions simply the result of a predetermined sequence of events which necessitate that a particular action occur? Are you free and morally responsible to love your family, or to not cheat in that exam? Are you free to keep reading this chapter? For many, the answer seems obvious: 'Of course I have the ability to freely choose in those situations!' The existence of free will appears to be the most basic view of reality.

However, such an admission is very troubling for those who deny the existence of the soul and hold to a naturalistic view of mankind. Why? Because in a completely materialistic worldview, humans are simply physical products of the physical world around them. The mind is simply the product of the brain, an organ governed by the natural laws. As Richard Dawkins has said, 'We believe that human brains, though they may not work in the same way as man-made computers, are surely governed by the laws of physics.'[41] Or as evolutionary psychologist Steven Pinker proclaims, 'Science is showing that what we call the soul—the locus of sentience, reason and will—consists of the information-processing activity of the brain, an organ governed by the laws of biology.'[42] If this is so, and we simply live in a universe where everything, including our brains, is operating in accordance with physical laws, then there cannot be such a concept as human free will. Free will is an illusion. This view is known technically by the term 'biological determinism' and it currently dominates much of the popular scientific landscape, due in part to the stranglehold that the naturalistic worldview has on science. Evolutionist William Provine spells this out clearly: 'Humans are comprised only of heredity and environment, both of which are deterministic. There is simply no room for the traditional concepts of human free will . . . so from my perspective as a naturalist, there's not even a possibility that human beings have free will.'[43]

It is important to remember that, although many secular scientists and academics push either a hard or a soft form of determinism as a somewhat scientific viewpoint, it is in fact a philosophical one. It cannot be tested by experimentation or observed in the laboratory. It is a belief based on the *a priori* assumption that human beings do not have free will. The fact that free will seems to be such an obvious fact of reality must be explained away. However, attempts to explain it away fall on the side of either nature (biology) or nurture (environment), and both have failed to provide a satisfactory account of reality that can replace human free will or provide convincing evidence against it.

BIBLICAL FREEDOM

The Bible records that when God first created humans, He gave them the ability to make free choices, thus displaying at least a degree of genuine freedom. This freedom is not an absolute freedom, as it must operate within the parameters that God has set, but it is an ability to make genuinely free choices. Actually, much of the Bible seems to be based upon the principle that humans are morally responsible for their free choices. God said to Adam and Eve, 'You are free to eat from any tree in the garden; but you must not eat from the tree of the knowledge of good and evil, for when you eat from it you will certainly die' (Genesis 2:16–17 NIV). And Paul writes in the book of Hebrews that 'if we go on sinning deliberately [wilfully] after receiving the knowledge of the truth, there no longer remains a sacrifice for sins' (Hebrews 10:26).

God desires that all people should be saved and come to a knowledge of the truth (1 Timothy 2:3–4). This means that humans have a free choice to accept God's wonderful offer of salvation and to have a relationship with Him. Of course, if this relationship is predicated upon a genuinely free choice, then the possibility of choosing to reject this offer also exists. Jesus wept over the city of Jerusalem because they were unwilling to accept him: 'O Jerusalem, Jerusalem, the city that kills the prophets and stones those who are sent to it! How often would I have gathered your children together as a hen gathers her brood under her wings, *and you were not willing*!' (Matthew 23:37). The early Church Father Irenaeus (c. AD 120–200), a disciple of Polycarp, who was himself a disciple of the apostle John, understood this verse to be expressing the concept of the free agency of mankind: 'This expression, "How often would I have gathered thy children together, and thou wouldest not", set forth the ancient law of human liberty, because God made man a free [agent] from the beginning, possessing his own power, even as he does his own soul, to obey the behests of God voluntarily, and not by compulsion of God.'[44] Irenaeus went on to explain that the reason we have free will is because we are created in the image of God, who is Himself free: 'because man is possessed of free will from the beginning, and God is possessed of free will, in whose likeness man was created, advice is always given to him to keep fast the good, which thing is done by means of obedience to God.'[45]

Free will is to be expected if mankind is the product of divine creation, made to reflect the Creator in distinct ways, but it remains an enigma for the materialist who believes only in the existence of the physical.

MALE AND FEMALE

This exploration of human identity would be incomplete without mentioning one area that is vitally important to our identity: gender. Genesis 1:27 says that God created man in His image, but goes on to state that He created them male and female. Thus, our gender is sacred. It is an integral component of our humanity, and this verse implies that men and women are distinct creations of God. This means that while women and men are equal in value and worth, they are not identical. It is vital to understand this. Both are created in the image of God, yet they are each given the privilege of fulfilling roles that the other cannot. There is a complementary design and beauty in men and women that contributes to the fullness of human identity. This truth is fundamental not only to the question of humanity, but also to the message of Christ.

The distinction of male and female in the created order is there by deliberate design. It teaches us something that is ultimately much more profound than just a good model of relationships in this life: it teaches us theological truths as a picture of Christ and His church. In Genesis 2:24, after describing the creation of Eve, the Bible gives this instruction: 'Therefore a man shall leave his father and his mother and hold fast to his wife, and they shall become one flesh.' In the New Testament, the apostle Paul quotes this verse and then says, 'This mystery is profound, and I am saying that it refers to Christ and the church' (Ephesians 5:32). The concept of two people, male and female, coming together in marriage as one flesh is a picture of the union and communion of Christian people (the church) and their Lord (Christ); it beautifully exemplifies Christ's covenant commitment to His people. This is why one of the names of the church in the Bible is the 'bride of Christ'. The distinction that we see in the created order between male and female reflects that found between God and humanity, and the unity of one flesh created through marriage reflects the deep desire that God has to be united with his people for ever.

This is why the Christian ethic of monogamous, lifelong marriage is so important. Far from being a way to limit people, it is safeguarding not only the people involved but also the sacred and beautiful picture that the marriage covenant gives us about the love of God for His people. This picture only works when the binary male–female design is retained; it is only as the two different, but complementary, sexes join together in a union that the image of God (as specified in the created order of Genesis) is accurately represented. The picture given to us in marriage also teaches us about the future. The glorious and beautiful event at the end of the Bible is a marriage celebration. At the marriage supper of the Lamb (Revelation 19:9), the eternal union between Jesus and His bride, the church, will be celebrated by all the heavenly hosts. This final event is what it all points to; and when the fulfilment has arrived, the earthly shadow can pass away. That is why we see that in the age to come there will be no marriage (Mark 12:25); the shadow is no longer needed in the glorious light of the reality! The reality can only be fully consummated with the redemptive work of Jesus Christ who saves and redeems those who place their faith in Him. The image of marriage, based upon the male–female distinction, points to Christ for its final fulfilment.

IT'S YOUR CHOICE?

In addition to the theological truths above, which help explain the rationale behind God's unique design of the two different genders, there are also many sociological aspects (and, unfortunately, even political aspects) that enter this discussion on identity. The binary male–female concept of gender is currently being dismantled by popular culture. Under the guise of supporting those who identify as transgender, a real but very small minority, support for affirming male–female distinctions is deliberately being eroded. This is dangerous and will create huge confusion as it relates to individual identity. There has been a move to try to separate the idea of gender from biology. In effect, this leaves people in the unusual situation of, for example, having to affirm a person who may feel that 'she' is a woman, yet lives in a male body, which is now the 'wrong' body. Therefore, rather than provide support and assistance that affirms the beauty of such a person's real biological gender, our culture increasingly encourages them to experiment with living as their 'chosen' gender and maybe trying to change their gender through surgery, or even refusing to identify with any gender regardless of the biological reality.

According to this narrative, our gender identity is nothing more than a social construct that is fluid and unrelated to what our biology indicates. This seriously misguided notion creates a huge divide—as if it were possible (it is not)—between a person's psyche (soul) and a person's body, playing them off against each other. This sort of unnatural dissection will result in people with a fractured identity who are constantly striving for a holistic unity to their personhood, but who ultimately fail to achieve it. It will lead to resentment towards the body for being out of step with a person's perceived (or chosen) gender identity. The confusion that such a splintered understanding of humanity will produce is already evident in the younger generation. They not only have to deal with the normal challenges of adolescence and puberty, but also must now decide their gender by choosing an option from the available buffet of pre-selected gender identities. An example of this occurred in September 2016 in an interview with a child of ten on BBC Radio 4. The child self-identified as having a non-binary gender—that is, the child identified not with either male or female, but with both. Although 'Leo' was actually born a girl, she feels that she is more boy. The mother was on hand to provide confused listeners with a better explanation of this ten-year-old's psyche: 'Leo is definitely not a girl. Leo is more boy than girl . . . but he's not, like a lot of transgender people, a male mind who happened to be born in a female body. He's a non-binary mind who happened to be born in a female body.'[46] Without minimizing the reality that this young child was struggling with various issues which need to be taken seriously, are such statements representative of a ten-year-old? Is this not more suggestive of the current cultural ideology being pushed upon young people, right down to the language and terminology being employed? Such constructs seem to be absorbed from the top down.

NOTHING NEW UNDER THE SUN

Although many in our culture today see this attitude as a new and liberating progression—that we are emerging from the shackles of centuries-old tradition—it is actually a throwback to the ancient Greeks. Ancient Greek thought was heavily influenced by the teaching of the famous philosopher Plato, who taught that the spiritual world was good and the physical world was bad. In Greek thought, the soul, the spiritual element, was the real 'you', but this was imprisoned in a perishing physical body. One day, at death, the soul would be released to the realm of the spirits. Such an understanding impacted the way the Greeks behaved, leading them to argue that what you did with the body was not important as it was destined to perish anyway. This usually resulted in the gross sexual immorality for which the Graeco-Roman world was infamous and to which our culture seems to be keenly making a return.

When the message of the gospel started to spread amongst the Greek population, some of this Platonic mindset crept into the church. Some people envisioned the Judaeo-Christian concept of salvation as Platonic liberation of the soul from the body. We see the apostle Paul condemning the view of the Corinthian church that engaging in sexual acts with prostitutes was OK as it involved only the physical body (1 Corinthians 6:13–16). In later Christianity we see the opposite extreme that also traced its roots to Platonic thought: the monastic idea of denying the body physical pleasures such as sex and marriage, or punishing the body physically to stop it sinning. Both extremes represent a very low view of the body, a view which has been inherited not from the biblical teaching about humanity but from Greek dualism.

Such a view is not what we find in the Bible. As Vaughan Roberts explains, 'As God's creatures we are not simply souls trapped in human bodies. He made us as physical beings; we are embodied creatures.'[47] The apostle Paul says, 'your body is a temple of the Holy Spirit' (1 Corinthians 6:19), and 'everything created by God is good' (1 Timothy 4:4). This means that the body and the soul, although distinct in one way, are unified in our being in such a way that they are indivisible—quite contrary to Greek thought. As a gift of God, the body should be treated as integral to our being, and, as something that God created, it should be seen as very good. The current thinking behind the 'gender revolution' seems to be a derivative of this Greek view that separates the psyche from the body and allows for the anti-intuitive concept that the 'real you' is how you choose to identify regardless of the biological reality. It is true that we are living in what is termed 'a fallen creation', such that our bodies can be physically affected by disease and bodily deformities, and cognitive dissonance may exist between what our minds feel and what is true, but such situations cannot be rectified by offering people a false perception of reality.

BIOLOGICAL REALITY

Is there any basis for acknowledging extra genders in addition to male and female? Or even for the idea that a person can be both male and female simultaneously based upon their own perception of reality? There is none in the world of reality that is based upon observable facts. A person's gender is determined biologically by either the presence or the absence of the Y sex chromosome. A male always inherits a Y sex chromosome from his father and an X chromosome from his mother. A female inherits an X chromosome from her father and another from her mother. Males are therefore XY and females XX. This means that, barring the rare anomalies during meiosis (cell division), each of us has received either an X or a Y chromosome from our father and therefore our gender is biologically determined and written into the very fabric of our being, because these X and Y chromosomes are contained in every cell of our body.[48] Gender is therefore seen, quite rightly, as being pivotal, at the most fundamental level, in determining who we are. This means that attempts to change gender are really just external cosmetic changes and do nothing to change our actual genetic make-up. Equally, encouraging people to affirm the concept of gender fluidity could, in the long run, contribute to even more confusion in the area of human identity.

The reality is that, as human beings, we are all embodied creatures, whether male or female. We are body and soul, possessing inherent worth, dignity and value; and we are created equal in the image of God. This is a key truth that will set people free to really understand who they are!

Notes

1. Friedrich Nietzsche, *The Will to Power* (New York: Vintage, 1968), p. 401.
2. Ravi Zacharias, *Can Man Live without God* (Dallas: Word, 1994), pp. 26–27.
3. Aleksandr Solzhenitsyn, 'Men Have Forgotten God', The Templeton Address, 1983, http://orthochristian.com/47643.html.
4. Ibid.
5. Rob Cooper, 'Forcing a Religion on Your Children Is as Bad as Child Abuse, Claims Atheist Professor Richard Dawkins', *Mail Online*, 22 April 2013, http://www.dailymail.co.uk/news/article-2312813/Richard-Dawkins-Forcing-religion-children-child-abuse-claims-atheist-professor.html.
6. From *The Root of All Evil*, a television documentary on Channel 4 in January 2006.
7. Charles Darwin, 'Notebook C', in Paul Barrett et al. (eds), *Charles Darwin's Notebooks, 1836–1844: Geology, Transmutation of Species, Metaphysical Inquiries* (Ithaca: Cornell University Press, 1987), p. 300.
8. Stephen J. Gould, *Wonderful Life: The Burgess Shale and the Nature of History* (New York: W. W. Norton, 1989), p. 44.
9. Johann Hari, 'Peter Singer: Some People Are More Equal Than Others', *Independent* online, 1 July 2004, accessed 14 November 2017, http://www.independent.co.uk/news/people/profiles/peter-singer-some-people-are-more-equal-than-others-551696.html.
10. E. O. Wilson and Michael Ruse, 'The Evolution of Ethics', *New Scientist* 108, no. 1478 (17 Oct. 1985): 50–52.
11. W. Provine, 'Evolution and the Foundation of Ethics', *MBL Science* 3, no. 1: 25–29. Cited by P. E. Johnson, *Darwin on Trial*, 2nd edn (Downers Grove, IL: InterVarsity Press, 1993), p. 127.
12. Margaret Thatcher, Speech to the General Assembly of the Church of Scotland, 21 May 1988.
13. John Calvin, *Institutes of the Christian Religion*, trans. Henry Beveridge (Peabody, MA: Hendrickson, 2008), p. 4.
14. The philosophical term for this is 'substance dualism'.

15 Paul Copan, *How Do You Know You're Not Wrong?* (Grand Rapids: Baker, 2005), p. 96.

16 Daniel Dennett, *Freedom Evolves* (New York: Viking, 2003), p. 1.

17 Keith Ward, *The Big Questions in Science and Religion* (West Conshohocken, PA: Templeton, 2008), p. 28.

18 Joseph LeDoux, *Synaptic Self: How Our Brains Become Who We Are* (Harmondsworth: Penguin, 2002), p. 324.

19 Thomas Nagel, *Mind and Cosmos: Why the Materialist Neo-Darwinian Conception of Nature Is Almost Certainly Wrong* (Oxford: Oxford University Press, 2012), p. 35.

20 Jerry Fodor, 'The Big Idea: Can There Be a Science of Mind?', *Times Literary Supplement*, 3 July 1992, p. 5.

21 Colin McGinn, *The Mysterious Flame* (New York: Basic, 1999), pp. 13–14.

22 J. P. Moreland, in Lee Strobel, *The Case for a Creator* (Grand Rapids: Zondervan, 2007), p. 264.

23 Immanuel Kant, *Kant's Critique of Practical Reason and Other Works on the Theory of Ethics* (New York/London: Macmillan, 1896; repr. London: Forgotten Books, 2012), p. 313.

24 C. S. Lewis, *Mere Christianity* (London: Harper Collins, 2002), p. 8.

25 Ibid., p. 13.

26 Zacharias, *Can Man Live without God*, p. 182.

27 Lewis, *Mere Christianity*, p. 25.

28 Ibid., p. 30.

29 Ibid., p. 31.

30 Ibid.

31 In debate with Frank Turek. 'Examine Reality (Frank Turek vs. David Silverman)', YouTube, 17 August 2017, https://www.youtube.com/watch?v=RzP07nEwNP8.

32 In Wilson and Ruse, 'The Evolution of Ethics', pp. 51–52.

33 Richard Dawkins, *River out of Eden* (New York: Basic, 1992), p. 133.

WHO AM I?

34 Richard Dawkins, *A Devil's Chaplain: Selected Writings* (London: Phoenix, 2004), p. 13.

35 Friedrich Nietzsche, *Twilight of the Idols and the Anti-Christ* (London: Penguin, 2003 [1889]), pp. 80–81.

36 '4. Crimes in the Conduct of War', 'Second Day: Wednesday, 21st November 1945', in *The Trial of German Major War Criminals, Sitting at Nuremburg, Germany*, Vol. 1, p. 78, The Nizkor Project, http://www.nizkor.org/hweb/imt/tgmwc/tgmwc-01/tgmwc-01-02-07.html.

37 'One Hundred and Eighty-Eighth Day: Saturday, 27th July, 1946', in *ibid.,* '16th July to 27th July 1946', Vol. 19, p. 470, The Nizkor Project, http://www.nizkor.org/hweb/imt/tgmwc/tgmwc-19/tgmwc-19-188-08.shtml.

38 'One Hundred and Eighty-Seventh Day: Friday, 26th July, 1946', in *ibid.,* '16th July to 27th July 1946', p. 383, The Nizkor Project, http://www.nizkor.org/hweb/imt/tgmwc/tgmwc-19/tgmwc-19-187-01.shtml.

39 Alison Flood, '"Post-Truth" Named Word of the Year by Oxford Dictionaries', *The Guardian,* 15 November 2016, https://www.theguardian.com/books/2016/nov/15/post-truth-named-word-of-the-year-by-oxford-dictionaries.

40 'Braveheart: The Speech of William Wallace', 1000 Diamonds, https://1000diamonds.wordpress.com/2010/06/02/braveheart-the-speech-of-william-wallace/.

41 Richard Dawkins, quoted by Mario Beauregard and Denyse O'Leary, *The Spiritual Brain* (New York: HarperOne, 2007), p. 118.

42 Steven Pinker, *The Blank Slate: The Modern Denial of Human Nature* (New York: Viking, 2002), pp. 10–11.

43 William Provine, in Russell Stannard (ed.), *Science and Wonders* (London: Faber, 1996), p. 60.

44 Irenaeus of Lyons, *Against Heresies* 4.37.1, http://www.earlychristianwritings.com/text/irenaeus-book4.html.

45 Ibid., 4.37.4.

46 '"I'm Not a Boy or a Girl. I'm Both": A Ten-Year-Old Talks about Being Gender Non-Binary', 'iPM: We Start with Your Stories', BBC Radio 4, http://www.bbc.co.uk/programmes/p0483lnc.

47 Vaughan Roberts, *Transgender* ([Epsom]: Good Book Company, 2016), p. 38.

48 Except for anucleated cells (ones which lose the nucleus as a normal part of development), e.g. red blood cells.

5 I am flawed

Not long ago, while scrolling through the feed on a social media account, I stumbled upon a humorous comic strip. It depicted two men in an office, sitting at opposite sides of a large desk. One man was clearly the boss and the other, drawn to look younger and less experienced, was being interviewed. The interviewee handed his CV to the man across the table, and the final scene showed the boss looking at the CV and saying, 'Made in the image of God . . . Impressive!', with the younger man grinning smugly. Being made in the image of God is indeed very impressive, in many ways.

However, there is more to the story than this. There is a further instalment in this story of humanity that does not sit so well with us. The truth is that we are broken and flawed in many ways, and the image of God in us has been corrupted. This corruption came through the entrance of sin into the world and it has impacted every aspect of creation. 'Sin', an unpopular term today, simply means rebellion against God and transgression of his commandments (1 John 3:4). The original Hebrew word implies missing the mark, with 'the mark' being the perfect will of God. It is like when an archer fires an arrow at a target, but, instead of hitting the bull's-eye, the arrow falls short of the target; it misses the mark.

Someone once asked Billy Graham, 'What is the definition of sin?' He replied, 'A sin is any thought or action that falls short of God's will. God is perfect, and anything we do that falls short of His perfection is sin.'[1]

All people are born sinners by nature; this means we are born in opposition to God and separated from Him. We would probably all readily admit that if the bull's-eye is the perfect will of God, then we have often fallen short in our behaviour and actions; we have sinned and missed the mark. The Bible is correct when it asserts that 'all have sinned and fall short of the glory of God' (Romans 3:23).

BUT WHY ARE WE LIKE THIS?

To understand why we are like this, we need to go back to the beginning of mankind's history and examine an event known as the Fall of Man. This event is recorded for us in Genesis 3 and is arguably one of the most important events in Scripture for us to grasp. It is here that we see the entrance of pain, suffering and death into the world God created. All that we observe and know about the world today is understood through the lens of the Fall in Genesis 3. It was here in the Garden of Eden that everything changed! To fully appreciate the impact this had it must be understood that, in God's original finished creation, there was no evil and no death; it was described as 'very good' (Genesis 1:31). Given that this declaration came from God, who is Himself good, holy and the very source of life, it is reasonable to infer that there was no such thing as death and suffering in the world at this point.

This has been the historic position of Christian theology and it finds biblical support in Paul's letter to the Corinthians, where he describes death as 'the last enemy to be destroyed' (1 Corinthians 15:26). Surely God's declaration of the whole creation as 'very good' could not have included something later referred to as an 'enemy'? This is the environment that was created for mankind, at this stage housing only the original people God created, Adam and Eve, who

> stood in a more direct relation to God, their Creator, than any other man has ever done . . . their hearts were pure, their discernment clear, their intercourse with God direct, . . . they were surrounded by gifts just bestowed by Him, and could not excuse themselves on the ground of any misunderstanding of the divine prohibition, which threatened them with the loss of life in the event of disobedience.[2]

HISTORICAL ADAM

It has become popular in some contemporary theological circles to doubt the historicity of Adam. It is argued that the scriptural account in Genesis is not to be taken as an actual historical record of what happened, but merely as a literary device used to illustrate the deeper theological and moral truths. Unfortunately, such an approach contradicts basic interpretative techniques that are used to understand the text. The book of Genesis is a unified whole and the history in the earlier chapters (1–11) cannot be divorced from that found in the later chapters (12–50), which are generally not under such scrutiny. The literary style of the two 'parts' is the same and the use of a particular construction of Hebrew verbs throughout Genesis indicates that all of it is to be taken as historical narrative and not as poetry, as some assert.

The detailed genealogies in Genesis 5 and Genesis 11 connect Adam to the other characters of the Bible, such as Noah and Abraham. If genealogical records begin with a 'mythical literary construct', they are completely useless. Even in the New Testament, when considering the family lineage of Jesus, we see a record that goes back to Adam (Luke 3:23–38); this is surely meant to be historical, unless Jesus was descended from a literary metaphor! The apostle Paul uses the historicity of Adam to teach the theological truth that it was Adam's sin that brought death and suffering into the world (Romans 5:12; 1 Corinthians 15:21–22). The writers of the New Testament consistently refer to the early history of Genesis as real history, and there is no clear biblical reason for us to contradict them.

So the human story began back in the Garden of Eden, at a time before the world was corrupted by sin. No actual evil existed at this time, for mankind had not encountered anything but the delight and joy of being in the presence of the Lord. God's design for mankind was that His creatures would be able to truly love—and true love necessitates the freedom to choose. God created man and woman with the power of contrary choice. This meant that they could freely and honestly enter a loving relationship with God without coercion or any sort of pre-programming on behalf of God, but it also meant that they would have the power to make a choice that would go contrary to God's intended design. This is the high cost of true love. And it was Satan, having already abused his own power of contrary choice, who sought the opportunity to exploit this same possibility in Adam and Eve.

God placed Adam in the garden, giving him the responsibility of cultivating and managing it (Genesis 2:15). He instructed that Adam could eat from any tree in the garden, except the tree of the knowledge of good and evil. God specified that eating from this tree would be a direct violation of His authority, and the consequence would be death (2:17). Every good thing was before the first two humans at this point. The only thing they had to avoid was the desire to experience what God had forbidden. Now we see how Satan works: he deceives us, causing us to disobey the commandments of God. In Genesis 3:1 we see the serpent, the animal used by Satan as a vehicle for his deceptive ends, asking Eve a question: 'Did God actually say, "You shall not eat of any tree in the garden"?'

THE TEMPTATION

Satan is described as being 'more crafty than any other beast of the field', and here we see him subtly creating doubt about God's word in the mind of Eve. In the Hebrew, the question from Satan is more forceful, expressing surprise at the unreasonableness of God's command, perhaps along the lines of: 'Is it really a fact that God has stopped you eating from all the trees?' Satan also twists the command from God, making it seem more difficult than it really was by implying that God had restricted them from enjoying all the trees in the garden when, in fact, His prohibition concerned only the one tree. And it was a prohibition that was instituted to protect them, not restrict them.

In the garden the serpent now advances his deceptive ploy and exchanges the clear and simple command of God for a lie. In Genesis 3:4 the serpent says to Eve, 'You will not surely die.' This small sentence is the first lie recorded in the Bible and it is a full-frontal attack on the word of God, being an outright contradiction of what God had previously stated. This is why Satan is called 'the father of lies' (John 8:44). However, Satan goes further than just contradicting the word: he maligns the character of God in the process. He continues, 'For God knows that when you eat of it your eyes will be opened, and you will be like God, knowing good and evil' (3:5). The implication here is that God was restricting them from this one tree in order to hold them back, to make sure that they did not get the same knowledge He had, and thus become like Him.

The temptation proved too strong for Eve, and she succumbed to Satan's deceptive strategy. We can learn a very important lesson about temptation, and the three primary avenues through which we are tempted, from this account. Genesis 3:6 first records that Eve 'saw that the tree was good for food', then, secondly, that 'it was a delight to the eyes', and, finally, that it was 'desired to make one wise'. Elsewhere in the Bible, these three areas of temptation are listed as coming from the world, not from God. For example, 1 John 2:16 reads, 'For all that is in the world—the desires of the flesh and the desires of the eyes and pride in possessions [or 'pride of life', NIV]—is not from the Father but is from the world.' The desires of the flesh, the desires of the eyes and the pride of life perfectly match the temptations to which Eve surrendered in the Genesis account; they are even listed in the same order. It is in these same areas that we are tempted today. The flesh is often aroused by the eyes, those windows into the soul. The poet William Blake said it this way in his poem *The Everlasting Gospel*:

This life's dim windows of the soul
Distorts the heavens from pole to pole
And leads you to believe a lie
When you see with, not through, the eye.

With the eyes we often view things that are harmful, things that will corrupt and ultimately produce a craving for more. The Bible describes the deeds of the flesh in this way: 'the works of the flesh are evident: sexual immorality, impurity, sensuality, idolatry, sorcery, enmity, strife, jealousy, fits of anger, rivalries, dissensions, divisions, envy, drunkenness, orgies, and things like these' (Galatians 5:19–21). Yet it is the lusts of our own hearts that cause us to capitulate to the many temptations we find around us, and, just like Eve, we fall for the lie. The book of James says that 'each person is tempted when he is lured and enticed by his own desire' (James 1:14). When Eve was tempted by the devil, she made a choice to follow her own desires and her own interpretation of events. She placed her opinion above the word of God, which was Satan's desired end then and still is today. The correct response to the temptation would have been to fall back upon the already given command of God and to say to the tempter, 'You lie, for it is written . . .' In the New Testament (Matthew 4), there is an episode where we witness the devil seeking to tempt Jesus in the same manner. He again uses this three-pronged attack strategy. In response to every attempt of Satan, Jesus replies by quoting authoritatively the word of God.

The narrative in Genesis continues, saying that after Eve had disobeyed she gave some of the fruit to her husband, Adam, 'who was with her' (Genesis 3:6), and he ate too. The difference between what Adam did and what Eve did is that, whereas Eve was deceived into temptation by Satan, Adam was not: the Bible records that Adam was not deceived (1 Timothy 2:13–14). This means that when Adam ate the fruit, he was engaging in an act of wilful disobedience and rebellion against God. This is why in the New Testament, Adam is the one held responsible for introducing sin into the creation (Romans 5:12).

THE TRAGIC RESULTS

The consequences of this rebellion were felt immediately in the creation. The text records that 'the eyes of both were opened, and they knew that they were naked' (Genesis 3:7). They were ashamed of their nakedness for the first time and they 'hid themselves from the presence of the LORD God' (3:8). This is perhaps the most tragic statement in the Bible, and it shows the devastating consequences of sin. Sin causes fellowship with God to be broken. Their eyes 'were opened', just as Satan had promised, but the results were not what they had expected. The world and the devil promise many things through temptations and lies, but the reality is often far different from what is promised. Adam and Eve's perfect communion with their Creator had been severed by disobedience. Yet broken fellowship with God entailed much more: God had told them that death would ensue. Spiritual death was the immediate consequence, and the process of physical death began with it. From now on, all humans born from Adam would be born spiritually dead—that is, with a sin nature that separated them from God. The book of Romans says that 'sin came into the world through one man, and death through sin, and so death spread to all men because all sinned' (Romans 5:12).

As God pronounced judgement on Adam, Eve and the serpent (Genesis 3:14–19), it was clear that everything in the created realm would be impacted by this tragedy, as many events in the rest of Genesis imply. Satan was judged, and the serpent became the age-long adversary of man. Humanity was affected in many ways. The man and woman's relationship to each other was changed for ever, as was their relationship to God and the creation itself (Romans 8:18–25). The very ground was cursed in judgement, pain and suffering, signified by the presence of 'thorns and thistles' which would now be part of the human experience; and the process of surviving would produce 'sweat' and tears. Life would be hard in many ways in what was now a hostile environment outside the luxuries of Eden. Ultimately, the prospect of death would cast a long shadow over the corridors of human history.

DR JEKYLL AND MR HYDE

The classic gothic novella written by Robert Louis Stevenson, *The Strange Case of Dr Jekyll and Mr Hyde*, provides a fascinating exploration of the dual nature of man. In the novel, which is set in Victorian England, Dr Jekyll is a respected scientist and a valued member of high society, yet he hides a dark, immoral side to his personality. Tired of the constant battle within his nature, he theorizes that if he could somehow separate the two personas, he would then be able to destroy the evil one. In his laboratory, he concocts a potion to separate these two natures. When Dr Jekyll ingests the potion, his immoral nature is revealed in a hideous transformation that changes him into another person, Mr Hyde. The potion can also transform Mr Hyde back into Dr Jekyll. As the story progresses we see him flitting between these two personas, the sinful escapades of Mr Hyde contrasting with the actions of the benevolent Dr Jekyll.

It is not long before we see Dr Jekyll succumb to the intoxicating power that this double life affords him. One morning, the unthinkable happens to Dr Jekyll: he wakes up as Mr Hyde without the use of the potion. As the story reaches a climax, the actions of Mr Hyde become more monstrous and he steadily gains control over Dr Jekyll. In a state of desperation, Dr Jekyll realizes that things have gone too far and decides never to take the potion again. This keeps Mr Hyde at bay for a short time, but then, in a moment of contemplation about the deeds of Mr Hyde and the pride he had in his actions as Dr Jekyll, he once again transforms into My Hyde. By this stage in the story the original potion used to transform Mr Hyde back into Dr Jekyll is running out and he gets people to search the city for certain ingredients. By the end of the story one ingredient has changed, and the original composition of the potion is no longer reproducible. Dr Jekyll seems to give in to Mr Hyde and loses control of his alter ego; in a final desperate act, he surrenders to Mr Hyde and chooses death. Dr Jekyll's friends break into his laboratory and find the body of Mr Hyde on the floor with a bottle of poison in his hand.

This short story offers some fascinating insights into the dual nature of man. Dr Jekyll even calls this duality 'a hard law of life that lies at the root of religion and is one of the most plentiful springs of distress'.[3] As we progress through the novel we see Dr Jekyll slowly discover that the evil part of his nature is, in fact, part of himself. In the final chapter, a sort of confession written by Dr Jekyll, he comments that he 'thus drew steadily nearer to the truth . . . that man is not truly one, but truly two . . . I saw that of the two natures that contended in the field of my consciousness, even if I could rightly be said to be either, it was only because I was radically both.'[4]

Curiously, elsewhere he describes how the allure of committing acts of immorality was such a powerful force within him that he was 'sold as a slave to my original evil', and that this new power, the ability to transform into Mr Hyde and sin recklessly, 'tempted me until I fell into slavery'.[5] So here we have a man with an immoral part of his nature described as a 'slave' to these passions and who knows that the only way to beat the nefarious Mr Hyde is by death. The end to this classic tale is poignant: 'God knows; I am careless; this is my true hour of death . . . Here then, as I lay down the pen and proceed to seal up my confession, I bring the life of that unhappy Henry Jekyll to an end.'[6]

The way out of slavery was by death! It is here that the parallels to the Christian gospel become clearer. The Bible describes humanity with a similar duality to that of Dr Jekyll. On the one hand, we are purposeful creations of a loving God, fashioned in His image; but, on the other hand, we are separated from Him by our rebellion and sin (Romans 3:23). Furthermore, no one is righteous (Romans 3:10); everyone is dead in sin (Ephesians 2:5), with a deceitful heart (Jeremiah 17:9). Our hearts are said to be the source of this sin (Matthew 15:8; James 4:1) and we are, in fact, slaves to sin (Romans 6:6, 17). The wages of sin is death (Romans 6:23). However, the amazing and glorious truth of the Christian message is that another has died in our place: Jesus died the death we deserve. This is the answer to our predicament. This one great act, the death of Jesus—the most important act in all history—made a way for all to be forgiven of their sins and to share in the new life that Christ offers. Christ rose again on the third day, defeating death, disarming principalities and powers, freeing all who trust in Christ from slavery to sin, and securing our eternal destiny by uniting us with Him. This radical transformation is what lies at the heart of the Christian gospel and it is utterly unique to the Christian faith: there is no one else who has done what Jesus did for us, no one who can come even close to offering what He does.

HOW DARE YOU CALL ME A SINNER!

Such is the indignation that might be levelled at someone who points out the above truths to people. How dare we deconstruct their positive self-image! They imply that we may inadvertently contribute to someone having low self-esteem. Society's obsession with self-esteem is readily apparent by perusing the shelves at any local bookstore. Many titles offer quick and easy steps to a better life, or a new you, or some other way to boost a flagging ego. The fact that so many books exist should, in and of itself, point us to the truth that something is not quite right. The mantra of the modern age is that we need to feed an ever-increasing desire for a positive self-image and self-acceptance. Negative thoughts and comments that seem to pull down a person's self-esteem are not welcome in this way of thinking. Yet the problems of self-image persist.

Occasionally a pious religious man will step into the fold and offer his view of humanity, focusing singularly on humanity as a miserable and wretched band of sinners, deserving of death. So which is it? Are we supposed to have a low self-image or a high self-image? We actually need to have the biblical understanding of ourselves, which, as we have seen, implies the wonderful truths indicating the great value God has placed on each individual person, yet at the same time means we need to confront seriously the aspects of humanity that are not so positive. The Bible is very clear that we human beings have a universal problem on our hands: the sin that has separated us from God. This should mean that any preference we have for personal exaltation and self-flattery is done away with, seeing that we are all the same in our fallen natures. Paradoxically, however, this fallen nature means that pride often raises its ugly head and tempts us to personal exaltation. This is why the Bible exhorts us to consider others as better than ourselves (Philippians 2:3) and not to think more highly of ourselves than we should (Romans 12:3).

This duality that consists within man is fiercely resisted yet at the same time it is an unavoidable conclusion. Malcom Muggeridge said, 'The depravity of man is at once the most empirically verifiable reality but at the same time the most intellectually resisted fact.'[7] He meant that every day we can look at the newspapers, the TV or those around us and witness the horrifying effects of the sinful nature of man. Yet, although this evidence is overwhelming, most people, when asked, still believe that they themselves are basically good. American Nobel Prize-winning author John Steinbeck eloquently describes the situation of mankind in his novel *The Log from the Sea of Cortez*:

> There is a strange duality in the human which makes for an ethical paradox. We have definitions of good qualities and of bad; not changing things, but generally considered good and bad

throughout the ages and throughout the species. Of the good, we think always of wisdom, tolerance, kindliness, generosity, humility; and the qualities of cruelty, greed, self-interest, graspingness, and rapacity are universally considered undesirable. And yet in our structure of society, the so-called and considered good qualities are invariable concomitants of failure, while the bad ones are the cornerstones of success . . . Perhaps no other animal is so torn between alternatives. Man might be described fairly adequately, if simply, as a two-legged paradox.[8]

TAKING RESPONSIBILITY

The Bible lays at the feet of man the responsibility for many of the calamities and instances of suffering experienced around the world. Jesus said, 'out of the heart come evil thoughts, murder, adultery, sexual immorality, theft, false witness, slander' (Matthew 15:19), and we quoted earlier the apostle Paul's words that 'the works of the flesh are evident: immorality, impurity, sensuality, idolatry, sorcery, enmity, strife, jealousy, fits of anger, rivalries, dissensions, divisions, envy, drunkenness, orgies, and things like these' (Galatians 5:19–21). The 'flesh' referred to is the sin nature, that propensity we have in us to participate in such acts. If we have ever engaged in any of the above, then the Bible declares that we are indeed sinners.

'Wait a minute,' you might be thinking, 'I might have been angry at someone before, but I have never done anything really bad, like murder; there are people who are far worse than me.' I'm sure that is true. There are probably plenty of people who have done things far more abhorrent than you have done. However, the fallacy with such a line of argument is that it makes other people the standard for comparison, and therefore there will always be those we can point to who fall beneath us, as well as those who would probably be ahead of us. The problem is that humanity is not the standard—God is! And He is a perfect, holy God who is unmatched in moral character and goodness, the one who is the very source of life. He is the standard by which the measurement must be made. In this case, it doesn't matter whether you are guilty of something deemed a 'major' sin or what we might consider a 'minor' sin. Any sin separates us from God (Isaiah 59:2), because as soon as that sin is committed we 'fall short of the glory of God' (Romans 3:23). James writes, 'For whoever keeps the whole law but fails *in one point* has become accountable for all of it' (James 2:10). Just one act, large or small, does the damage.

Picture yourself held up over a dark pit by a massive chain. There are huge, thick links at the top of the chain, which represent the most serious evils a man could commit, and, at the bottom of the chain, many thinner links, representing the everyday transgressions. What happens if one of the thick links is broken? You fall. But what happens if only one of the thin links is broken? You still fall! Similarly, the consequence of any sin is the same: separation from God.

'That's ridiculous!' you might be thinking. 'If the standard is so demanding, who on earth could meet it?' This is the right question to ask. For the truth is that no one can stand before God. There is no way to work your way up to God, or, to use our analogy, to fix your own chain. Humanly speaking, the situation in which mankind finds itself is utterly hopeless—without God. The only hope that mankind has is found in the person and message of Jesus Christ 'our hope' (1 Timothy

1:1). He is the only one who can offer hope in a hopeless world.

AS FAR AS YOU GO?

Sadly, for many who do not know Christ, this is often the point where the journey grinds to a halt. Although they are unique individuals created in the image of God, with all the inherent dignity that goes with it, their nature is fallen. This means that, without Christ, they are separated from God and missing out on all the fullness of human identity which can be theirs in Him. But there is so much more to explore—so much more that Christ has to offer. This is what we will examine in the rest of this book.

Notes

1 'Billy Graham's Answer: What Is Sin? Are All Sins Equal in God's Eyes?', Billy Graham Evangelistic Association, 26 March 2014, https://billygraham.org/story/billy-grahams-answer-what-is-sin-are-all-sins-equal-in-gods-eyes/.

2 F. Delitzsch, in C. F. Keil and F. Delitzsch, *Biblical Commentary on the Old Testament*, Volume 1: *The Pentateuch* (Peabody, MA: Hendrickson, 2001), p. 96.

3 Robert Louis Stevenson, *Dr Jekyll and Mr Hyde* (London: Penguin, 2012), p. 57.

4 Ibid., p. 58.

5 Ibid., p. 62.

6 Ibid., p. 74.

7 Quoted in Ravi Zacharias, *Has Christianity Failed You?* (Grand Rapids: Zondervan, 2010), p. 64.

8 John Steinbeck, *The Log from the Sea of Cortez* (New York: Penguin, 1995), p. 80

6 I am redeemed

Old pirates, yes, they rob I
Sold I to the merchant ships
Minutes after they took I
From the bottomless pit . . .
Won't you help to sing
These songs of freedom?
'Cause all I ever have
Redemption songs
Redemption songs

(Bob Marley, 'Redemption Song')[1]

Bob Marley wrote the above words in 1980, and he died shortly after in 1981, due to complications with cancer. In this classic song, which was the last he ever recorded, we get to see the message that Marley wanted to leave to the world, a track that would sum up everything he believed in and stood for. His message was one of freedom, of redemption. Infused with a spirituality derived from his Rastafarian faith and applied to the tragic history of African slavery, Marley sang about redemption from physical slavery and from mental slavery and all forms of oppression. But although Marley's iconic song captured the mood of generations, it falls short of capturing the full meaning of biblical redemption. The language of redemption finds its origins in the pages of the Bible. It is true that the illustration of freedom from slavery gives us our picture of redemption, as we shall see below; but in the fuller sense it is about all of mankind being redeemed to God from slavery to sin.

TRAPPED AND HELPLESS

Sometimes in life it can feel as if the walls are closing in on all sides and the exit is nowhere to be seen. The daily pressures of living in a fallen world test us in many ways, sometimes in ways we least expect. We can create prisons out of our pain and find ourselves swallowed up in the face of the ever-encroaching darkness. Those who feel trapped in this way feel they have nowhere to turn; they long for something or someone to break into their darkness and lead them to freedom.

As we explored in the last chapter, mankind is fallen, separated from God and living in a sin-stained world. This fact is undeniable. However, usually the world misses the most important part of the message of Christianity, the part known as the 'good news'. There is a Redeemer who has come to free us from our slavery to sin—who has come to rescue us, represent us, forgive us, pay the ransom for us, and utterly deliver us from the kingdom of darkness. This Redeemer desires to emancipate us from shame, guilt and evil, and transfer us into the glorious kingdom of light. But to properly understand redemption, we first need to understand that we need redemption, that we are slaves in some way, and then acknowledge that there is a Redeemer. In the words of the popular worship song,

There is a redeemer
Jesus, God's own Son

Precious Lamb of God, Messiah
Holy One

(Melody Green, 1982)[2]

Tragically, many people place their destinies in the hands of those who cannot keep them, hoping to find solace in the temporary solutions offered by the world. They seek meaning and fulfilment in relationships or positions. But such things are nothing more than a way of providing temporal comfort to us slaves, things which can keep us from rising up and can provide us with a semblance of freedom; it is quite another thing to actually set the captives free. This requires a redeemer, a saviour!

FROM EGYPT TO THE PROMISED LAND

The story of mankind's redemption is etched deep into the annals of history, surfacing more acutely at different times and in different ways. The message of the Bible is often explained by dividing the narrative into three portions: Creation, Fall and Redemption. The first two actually take up very little space in the pages of Scripture but, by contrast, the theme of redemption runs like a crimson thread throughout the entire book. It weaves its way through history, infusing the lives of men and women with destiny and promise, giving meaning to the suffering, explaining the sacrifice of many, and displaying the promise of eternal glory that caused the faithful to cling to the God of Israel. Finally, this crimson thread became visible to the entire world when love ran red on the hill of Calvary all those years ago, accomplishing the greatest act of redemption ever known.

The language of redemption finds its origin in the story

of the exodus, an event commemorated to this day during the Jewish festival of Passover. In the second millennium BC the Israelite nation had become slaves in the land of Egypt. They were oppressed and in bondage to the Egyptians. God raised up a deliverer, Moses, who was charged with leading the Israelites out of Egypt. Moses confronted the pharaoh of the day, petitioning for him to let the Israelites go. Pharaoh's heart was hardened against Moses, who at the behest of God threatened Pharaoh with a series of plagues to punish the Egyptians for all they had done to the Israelites. The severity of the plagues gradually increased, yet still Pharaoh refused to let the Israelites go. The tenth and final plague to be brought on Egypt was the death of all the firstborn children in the land, after which the people of Israel were finally set free.

The Lord commanded his people to prepare for this event by performing several different rites in order that their households would escape the penalty of the plague. In Exodus 12 we read how the Israelites were instructed to take an unblemished lamb, and on the fourteenth day of the tenth month they were to kill this lamb at twilight. The blood of the lamb was then to be applied to the doorposts of their houses and the meat was to be consumed on the same evening along with unleavened bread and bitter herbs. God instructed them that this was 'the LORD's Passover' (Exodus 12:11) and that the blood was to be a sign for them: 'when I see the blood, I will pass over you, and no plague will befall you to destroy *you* when I strike the land of Egypt' (12:13). It was because this final plague caused such devastation in the land of Egypt that Pharaoh decided to free the slaves of Egypt. Moses then led the Israelites to freedom through the miraculous Red Sea crossing, after which they began their wilderness journey to the Promised Land.

This narrative provides the historical and theological backdrop for the redemption language used throughout the Bible. The Israelites were in 'slavery' in Egypt, and their emancipation from Egypt is described in terms of 'redemption', as the following verses illustrate:

> it is because the LORD loves you and is keeping the oath that he swore to your fathers, that the LORD has brought you out with a mighty hand and redeemed you from the house of slavery, from the hand of Pharaoh king of Egypt. (Deuteronomy 7:8)

> You shall remember that you were a slave in the land of Egypt, and the LORD your God redeemed you; therefore I command you this today. (Deuteronomy 15:15)

THE GREATER REDEMPTION

The New Testament uses this history to form a doctrinal foundation that can teach us about the redemption accomplished by the death of Christ. It is not possible to find one word that covers all that was accomplished on the cross, but we generally use the term 'salvation'. When used in this broad sense it usually includes all the salvific imagery that we find woven throughout the New Testament, particularly the doctrines of atonement and justification. 'Atonement' is a central theme in biblical theology and means that God has provided a way for man to come back into a harmonious relationship with Him. In the Old Testament, we see this prefigured by the many sacrifices that were used for atonement, and in the New Testament the reality is that people are brought into a right relationship with God through the atoning sacrifice of Christ on the cross.

'Justification' is the means by which this can be accomplished. It shows us how a person separated from a holy God can be declared righteous and accepted by Him. The term has legal implications and, theologically, it speaks to the fact that, on the cross, Christ took our sin and gave us His righteousness. This great exchange is one of the most important truths to grasp, especially as it impacts how you understand yourself in light of what Christ has done for you. If you have asked God for forgiveness and accepted Christ as your Saviour, then through the work of the cross you are declared righteous in God's sight. All the stains and violations of God's holy standards that you have accumulated in your life, along with the associated pain, brokenness, guilt and shame, are washed away by the blood of Christ. They are separated from you as far as the east is from the west, so that you are restored and renewed, and your life and identity are now hidden with God.

The Bible says, 'Therefore, if anyone is in Christ, he is a new creation. The old has passed away; behold, the new has come' (2 Corinthians 5:17). What a wonderful promise this is! How often we need a clean slate, a new start in life. The message of Christianity is unique and extraordinary: God does not just forgive; He also transforms the person who accepts Jesus into a new creature, washed and made whole by the work of Christ. Humanity was made to be in relationship with God, but without this relationship our identity better resembles the brokenness of Adam than the fullness of Christ for which we were made. To live with Christ is truly what it means to be human.

Redemption is closely linked to justification, but the two terms have a different focus. The teaching of redemption focuses not so much on the way a person is declared righteous before God, but on the fact that they are set free from slavery. The particular word groups used in the New Testament to teach about redemption highlight the major meanings for us, which in turn illuminate the theological conclusions that follow. The first word used for 'redeem' simply conveys the idea of purchase, buying something in the marketplace. The word was often used in reference to purchasing the freedom of a slave. The other group of words emphasizes that freedom is accomplished by the payment of a price, or a ransom. So the teaching of redemption we find in the New Testament speaks of purchasing a group of people out of slavery by paying a ransom.

For the Israelites who were redeemed out of slavery in Egypt, the price paid for their ransom was the blood of the Passover lamb. This is where the parallels get exciting. For humanity to be freed from their slavery to sin (Romans 6:17–20), there is also a price that must be paid. This is a price we could never pay, as no amount of silver or gold could ever purchase our freedom from sin. Instead, it requires a substitute, a perfectly sinless person to die in our place—one who could die the death that we deserved. Christ is that substitute. He is actually described as our Passover lamb (1 Corinthians 5:7) whose blood will set us free from slavery to sin. The Bible says that 'In him we have redemption through his blood, the forgiveness of our trespasses, according to the riches of his grace' (Ephesians

1:7). The blood of Christ was the ransom price: 'you were ransomed from the futile ways inherited from your forefathers, not with perishable things such as silver or gold, but with the precious blood of Christ, like that of a lamb without blemish or spot' (1 Peter 1:18). The blood of the Lamb has purchased our freedom. It is no coincidence that Jesus was crucified during the time when the Jewish people were celebrating the Passover and sacrificing lambs in remembrance of their delivery from Egypt. At that very time, God, by eternal decree, ordained that the true Passover Lamb would purchase redemption for all of humanity once and for all.

REDEMPTION AND YOU

Biblical redemption is a beautiful truth. The God of the universe came to earth to live as a perfect human in order that He could die in our place and save us. It cost Him everything. Every drop of His blood that was spilt upon the ground of Calvary that day was for you, to redeem you back to Himself. His pursuit of you took Him from the throne room of Glory, surrounded by the multitude of heavenly hosts, down to the hills of Jerusalem to be delivered into the hands of evil men. There He laid down His life. He was hated and despised, rejected and forsaken and nailed to the old rugged cross—all for *you*. This cross, this instrument of death, became the receipt that proves you have been purchased by God. That is the truth for human identity: if you are a believer in Jesus, you are a blood-bought individual, paid for with the highest currency known in the entire cosmos: the blood of God's own dear Son.

Seeing that such a high price was paid, it is all too easy for us as Christians to look at ourselves and maybe wonder whether God has somehow overpaid. After all, we still struggle with sin, we fail, and we continually let ourselves and God down. Surely this will change how God thinks of us? Surely, after we Christians have fallen back into the ways of the world so spectacularly, God will regret having paid so much for us? But the wonderful truth is that God saw every day of your life, every thought, every action and every deed, before you were even born. And even knowing all this, He ordained before the foundation of the earth (Revelation 13:8) that you would be one of His children.

So how does He see us now? Does he look at our performance to see whether we are acting as 'good' or 'bad' Christians? To think in such a way is to fail to grasp the glory of redemption and the truth of what He has done. God has freed you for ever. There is now no condemnation for those who are in Christ Jesus (Romans 8:1); you are so secure in Him that nothing can ever separate you from the love of God which is in Christ Jesus (Romans 8:39). He has promised that He will never leave you nor forsake you (Hebrews 13:5) and that no one is able to snatch you out of His hand (John 10:29). When the eternal Father looks at you, because your life is now 'hidden with Christ in God' (Colossians 3:3) and you are clothed with the righteousness of Christ, He looks at you with the same level of love with which He looks upon His own Son! Such love is so amazing, so divine, it demands our soul, our life, our all:

Were the whole realm of nature mine,
That were an offering far too small;

Love so amazing, so divine,
Demands my soul, my life, my all.

To Christ, who won for sinners grace
By bitter grief and anguish sore,
Be praise from all the ransomed race
Forever and forevermore.

(Isaac Watts, 'When I Survey the Wondrous Cross')[3]

NOTES OVERLEAF ➡

Notes

1 Redemption Song lyrics © Kobalt Music Publishing Ltd.

2 There Is a Redeemer lyrics © Universal Music Publishing Group, Capitol Christian Music Group.

3 Hymns and Spiritual Songs 1707.

7 I am loved

ROMEO
O, speak again, bright angel! For thou art
As glorious to this night, being o'er my head,
As is a wingèd messenger of heaven
Unto the white, upturnèd, wondering eyes
Of mortals that fall back to gaze on him
When he bestrides the lazy-puffing clouds
And sails upon the bosom of the air.

JULIET
O Romeo, Romeo! Wherefore art thou Romeo?
Deny thy father and refuse thy name.
Or, if thou wilt not, be but sworn my love,
And I'll no longer be a Capulet.[1]

William Shakespeare's classic sixteenth-century tale of forbidden love is considered one of the greatest love stories in all literature. It is certainly one of the most enduring. The play recounts the doomed exploits of two star-crossed lovers from rival feuding families, the Montagues and the Capulets. Romeo and Juliet, knowing their families will never allow them to marry, decide to wed in secret. However, the night before the wedding Romeo is involved in a duel with Juliet's cousin and kills him. He is exiled from the city on pain of death. Juliet is forced into an arranged marriage by her parents. She agrees to it because she plans to fake her death and escape with Romeo. Having ingested a sleeping potion which makes her appear dead, she is laid in the family crypt by her grieving family. Tragically, news of her plan does not reach Romeo in time and he finds her 'dead' in the tomb. Overcome with grief, he kills himself. When Juliet finally awakes from the potion she is devastated to find her lover dead next to her. She is distraught and decides to kill herself with Romeo's blade. The two families find them both dead at the tomb and are ultimately reconciled by their children's deaths, putting an end to the family feud. The play ends with these lines:

For never was a story of more woe
Than this of Juliet and her Romeo.[2]

SEEKING TRUE LOVE

Such poignant tales of forbidden love tug on the emotions of the audience, drawing them into the plot. History is littered with stories of love and tragedy. As well as Romeo and Juliet, a quick Internet search for the best love stories will reveal names like Antony and Cleopatra, or Elizabeth and Mr Darcy. Stories of romantic love are just as popular today as they have always been. Blockbuster movies and bestselling music still play on the public's desire for a good love story. The Western world's obsession with romantic love has meant that, in the minds of many, love is singularly associated with passion and desire. Love is often sold as the key to all happiness, and many young people dream of falling in love, pursuing it with such fervour that they are sometimes willing to jeopardize their own well-being.

Yet how many actually ask the question, 'What is love?' Should we try to understand love, or do we just want to feel love? The search for love is a universal phenomenon, something that seems to burn deep within the human heart, so it is important that we understand it. The vision of love so often portrayed in our culture through the media is heavily influenced by the romanticism of the eighteenth century. It is a love that focuses on feelings, on emotions and passions. Ironically, such a focus means that love can often become individualistic and selfish; it is no longer about others, but is primarily about ourselves. The pursuit of love can easily become the pursuit of the feelings you get when you are in love. This may be why there are so many stories of people falling in love and getting married at the height of passion but who, after a while, when the honeymoon period is gone, simply declare, 'I no longer love you.' And logically, if our concept of love is all about the feeling of 'falling in love', what is to stop the feeling of 'falling out of love'?

A true understanding of love, however, will involve much more than just feelings. Passion and desire are good when they are given legitimate expression within the environment for which they were created, but love cannot be reduced to this. As C. S. Lewis said, 'Love is not affectionate feeling, but a steady wish for the loved person's ultimate good as far as it can be obtained.'[3]

Love is a foundational element of human existence. The environment provided by loving parents or a spouse—the nurture, protection, encouragement and support that love provides—is something that every person longs for and deserves. You do not have to look far in this world to see the pain caused when those who are supposed to provide love fail to do so. There are times when love may be hard, may require sacrifice, and may be something you do not necessarily feel like giving. But, foundationally, love is a commitment and an action. Sometimes it will be accompanied by intense emotions and passions, but at other times it will require laying down your own desires for the sake of those you love. To love and to be loved has been called the highest virtue and the supreme ethic. Ultimately, love will affect how we behave, how we think and the value we place upon every human being. Love is intrinsic to who we are as human beings made in the image of God, and, as such, love finds its source, not in the mind of men, but in the mind of God.

GOD IS LOVE

In all mankind's imaginings and philosophical musings about love, one element is often missing: where does love come from? Why do we as human beings display this persistent quality of love? It cannot be explained as a wholly naturalistic concept, simply a result of physical processes and chemical reactions in the brain, or as some evolutionary phenomenon that developed to ensure the survival of our DNA. A full explanation of love cannot be provided in terms of matter and energy. It is a non-physical entity; therefore, it cannot be explained as simply a human survival mechanism, as great acts of self-sacrificial love should not exist in a universe that is indifferent to such notions.

The explanation offered by the Christian perspective provides the most comprehensive understanding of love. It gives both the source and the definition of love, as well as pointing to its ultimate demonstration. In Christianity, love is not merely something that happens between people, but is an attribute of God. This means that the source of love is God Himself; it is part of His nature, His very being. The Bible declares, 'Beloved, let us love one another, for love is from God, and whoever loves has been born of God and knows God. Anyone who does not love does not know God, because God is love' (1 John 4:7–8). Such a declaration is unique to the Christian faith and is perhaps one of the most sublime truths revealed to us in the Bible. It explains why love is such a dominant theme of the Christian faith. Probably the best-known verse in the Bible is John 3:16, which declares that 'God so loved the world . . .' When Jesus was asked what the greatest commandment in the law was, He responded with these classic words: 'You shall love the Lord your God with all your heart and with all your soul and with all your mind. This is the great and first commandment. And a second is like it: You shall love your neighbour as yourself. On these two commandments depend all the Law and the Prophets' (Matthew 22:37–40). These commandments state that loving God and loving others are the most important principles in the Bible. Where else in all the world do you find such a statement? The Bible declares that God is 'abounding in steadfast love and faithfulness' (Psalm 86:15), that He is 'rich in mercy', that He loves us with a 'great love' (Ephesians 2:4), that the 'steadfast love of the LORD never ceases' (Lamentations 3:22) and that 'as high as the heavens are above the earth, so great is his steadfast love towards those who fear him' (Psalm 103:11). Love is the motivation behind everything God does. Everything we read about in Scripture is moving towards the final consummation of love in heaven. His pursuit of you has one purpose: to get you to reciprocate that love. It is a pursuing love, one that longs to be lavished upon those He created to receive it.

AN UNCONDITIONAL LOVE

Our usual experience in this world is that we need to earn things, and our attitude towards love is often no different. The desire for love is so strong that people are willing to go to great lengths to try to elicit love from the people around them. This may be the love and praise that children desire from their parents, that feeling of acceptance and of knowing that they make them proud. There are often anguished cries from many who long for these affirmations from loving parents and don't get them: 'If I can just do what they want me to do, will they love me then? Why aren't they noticing me? What more can I do?'

Perhaps you have seen friends in a relationship try to change themselves, attempting to please the people they are involved with, in an effort to secure the other person's love and affection. Usually, they end up giving up part of their own character in the process, rather than having their own unique character encouraged and nurtured by the other. The tragedy with this attitude to love is that it all too easily creates insecurity, the confusion or loss of individual identity, and provides no foundation for lasting relationships. It treats love like a reflex that is conditional upon the correct response or behaviour. And often we project this flawed understanding of love onto God. We think, 'I've been really good today, I've followed all the rules, so God must be really pleased with me!'

What a travesty this is! The Bible shows that God's love is not revealed in such a temperamental and, dare I say it, human manner. God's love for the Christian is an unconditional love, one that cannot be coerced or earned, but simply exists. We do not deserve it, but it is freely given; it remains just as strong and real when we spurn it. He loves us even on those days when we fall into sin, on those days when we just want to be alone and at those times when we do not like anyone, not even ourselves. Nothing we do will cause Him to love us more, and nothing we can do will mean He loves us less. God's love is truly an unconditional love. What security we can take in this fact: that the Sovereign of the universe, the one who is high and lifted up, who dwells in eternity and holds the world in His hands, loves us with an everlasting love! It is this sort of love, freely given, freely received, that motivates us into service for the other. The Bible declares, 'We love because he first loved us' (1 John 4:19).

AN INFINITE AND ETERNAL LOVE

Could we with ink the ocean fill,
And were the skies of parchment made;
Were every stalk on earth a quill,
And every man a scribe by trade,
To write the love of God above
Would drain the ocean dry.
Nor could the scroll contain the whole,
Though stretched from sky to sky.

(F. M. Lehman, 'The Love of God', 1917)

Throughout human history, the heart of man has often been stirred to rapturous heights as it has contemplated the boundless and ineffable love of God. So endless are the beauties of divine love, it has served as the motivation for a million love songs, each penned to honour the God who loves us. It is more beautiful than any tongue can fully express and more infinite than any mind can fully comprehend. It is limitless in its scope, extending far above the highest heavens and reaching down to the lowest depths. It is inexhaustible in its supply: it has no beginning and no end. It is an eternal love, one that exists from everlasting to everlasting. It can be nothing else, for it springs forth from an eternal God who Himself is immeasurable in power and majesty and unsearchable in all His ways. This is the assurance we have that God will love us for all eternity. The apostle Paul declares that 'neither death nor life, nor angels nor rulers, nor things present nor things to come, nor powers, nor height nor depth, nor anything else in all creation, will be able to separate us from the love of God in Christ Jesus our Lord' (Romans 8:38–39).

A HOLY LOVE

One of the errors of our age has been to turn the love of God into nothing more than sloppy sentimentality by modelling it on the misguided way that love is construed in our culture. Unfortunately, 'love' has become a buzzword that can be used to justify almost anything. Therefore, it is now 'unloving' to disagree with someone, to express concern over someone's behaviour or to tell someone that what they are doing is harmful. It is unloving, so we are led to believe, to swim against the stream of popular culture. Somewhere along the line the meaning of love has changed from the exalted notion of always seeking the best for another person, to simply being an affirmation of their own (sometimes selfish) desires and will. We are told that God will not judge sin, for He is a God of love; God will just forgive me because He is a God of love; God does not mind if I do certain things because He is a God of love; and so the train of self-justifying mantras continues.

The love of God is not like this at all. It is a holy love. It is not controlled by emotions, but is employed in conjunction with the totality of His being. That means it operates in unison with His other attributes, including His holiness. The Bible frequently declares that God is holy (Isaiah 6:3). It is impossible to separate His holiness from His love; to do so would be to lessen the character of God and create a God of our own choosing. This is evident as it is typically the holiness and justice of God that people like to water down. However, trying to 'improve' the qualities of God (which cannot be improved) on the basis of the imagination of our minds is to create an idol of our imagination.

We need to be careful that we do not compartmentalize God's attributes and fall into the trap of thinking that in the Bible we see him operating according to these different parts or attributes. God is all of His attributes all of the time. It is good to study them individually, but only if we do so remembering that each attribute stands in relation to all the others; that to remove one, or alter one, is to make God less than what He is. So, because we know that God is holy, and also that God is love, we can conclude that His love is a holy love. A holy love will also seek to encourage holiness in the objects of that love. God is light (1 John 1:5), meaning that He is pure, undefiled, that nothing evil dwells in him; that is the essence of holiness. He is far above and beyond anything we can imagine. So this means that His holy love is a purifying love, one that seeks our well-being, that is not afraid to take corrective action if we stray (Hebrews 12:6). Ultimately, it is a love that seeks to conform us to His image, that 'we should be holy and blameless before him' (Ephesians 1:4). This means it is a love that will conform us to His truth. The apostle John, sometimes called the apostle of love, wrote these words about love: 'For this is the love of God, that we keep his commandments. And his commandments are not burdensome' (1 John 5:3).

A PRACTICAL LOVE

It is all very well describing these qualities of God's love, but sometimes we need to know what love looks like practically, and how love behaves. Many of us are familiar with what typically happens at a church wedding. Often you will hear the words of 1 Corinthians 13 read out at some point during the ceremony. This chapter, often simply called 'the love chapter', contains the most exquisite description of love in action that has ever been written:

> Love is patient and kind; love does not envy or boast; it is not arrogant or rude. It does not insist on its own way; it is not irritable or resentful; it does not rejoice at wrongdoing, but rejoices with the truth. Love bears all things, believes all things, hopes all things, endures all things. Love never ends.
>
> (1 Corinthians 13:4–8)

Early in my Christian walk I listened to a talk on this passage. The speaker asked us, his listeners, to read it, but every time we got to the word 'love', to substitute our own names. This exercise exposes how far short we fall of such a lofty description. In fact, I would be confident in betting that we all fail even at the first hurdle! The point of the exercise, though, was not to make us feel bad about how far short we fall of God's love, but to make us look to something bigger than ourselves. So the speaker asked us to read the passage again, this time inserting the name of Jesus in place of the word 'love'. If you do this, you will soon discover that the description of love fits perfectly as a description of the character and nature of Jesus. The most practical example we can look at in order to learn about love is the Lord Jesus, God incarnate, love incarnate.

GOD'S LOVE AND YOU

The love of God is on a continual, relentless pursuit. It is a pursuit as old as time itself, one that stretches back into eternity, to the very mind of God. It is a love that was there at the dawn of creation, that witnessed the creation of man and the first civilization. It has seen the rise and fall of great empires, revolutions and counter-revolutions, and witnessed great leaders rise to power only to fall, leaving only their footprints in the sands of time. Love was there when the Great Pyramids were built, and when the Parthenon and the Colosseum were the seats of world power. It has seen peace and war, plagues and famines, and witnessed man's greatest achievements and biggest failures. It was there when the Berlin Wall came down, when the *Titanic* sank, when man walked on the moon and when the Twin Towers fell. Divine Love has been there during every event in your life, all the time pursuing you, seeking you and calling you into relationship with Him, or taking you further into that existing relationship. It is the greatest love story ever written. It is God's story, but it is also your story; how the final chapter ends is up to you. If you do not know this love personally, will you continue to run from God, or will you accept Him and become a character in the greatest story ever told? If you already know Him, will you continue to search the depths of His love for you?

Many people in this world fail to receive the love they deserve from their fellow human beings, but God provided the greatest demonstration of His love for mankind two thousand years ago on a hill outside the city wall of Jerusalem. On that day Jesus was convicted as a criminal, although no wrongdoing on His part could be found. A crown of thorns was placed on His head, His back was scourged by a Roman whip and He was led out to the hill of Golgotha. There He was laid on His back while Roman centurions hammered nails through His hands and feet, fastening Him to the cross. Then, as they hoisted the cross up to a vertical position, the weight of His body caused Him to start to suffocate, until, hours later, with His last breath, He cried out, 'Father, forgive them, for they know not what they do.' The whole of history hinged upon this act: He divided human history into BC and AD, and nothing would ever be the same again. The Bible declares that, at the cross, 'God shows his love for us in that while we were still sinners, Christ died for us' (Romans 5:8). The cross of Christ stands for ever as a demonstration and testimony to the sacrificial love of God. It was on that cross that the Son of God died in our place, tasting the death that we deserved; it was here that the Father placed our sins upon Him, the innocent one, holy, spotless and unblemished. He was led as a lamb to the slaughter, yet it was a voluntary sacrifice, motivated by His love for us. He who knew no sin became sin for us, so that we might become the righteousness of God (2 Corinthians 5:21).

Think about this: Love came to earth, and we crucified Him! Yet still His love pursues us. What magnitude of love is this! It is no surprise that we find the apostle Paul praying that Christians 'may have strength to comprehend with all the saints what is the breadth and length and height and depth, and to know the love of Christ that surpasses knowledge' (Ephesians 3:18). Truly, this is a love that goes beyond our understanding into the transcendent realm of God. Yet for us down here on this earth, living in the midst of what is often a confusing and troubling world, we can look back to the cross, and *know* that we are loved, for God proved it all those years ago. Is it any wonder that the cross of Christ has become one of the most cherished symbols throughout the world? Even today we see people wearing a cross around their necks, most with little or no understanding that what they are wearing is an ancient torture device. But it was upon the cross that Jesus laid down His life, where He demonstrated the full extent of His love.

A SURE FACT OF HISTORY

There are times when we feel alone in this world, and many people truly are alone. People need to know that they are loved, and this is what the cross offers. Contrary to the critics, this is not a religious sentiment fobbed off on the masses to provide a false sense of comfort. The greatest demonstration ever given that you are loved by God was at the cross, and the crucifixion is an indisputable fact of history. The Christian faith is not simply a set of metaphysical beliefs or a vague set of spiritual principles for which people must take our word; it is history, a history that is undeniable. God entered history in His pursuit of mankind, and left His fingerprints all through it for us to find.

That the crucifixion is a historical fact is the consensus of modern historians who have examined the subject. The eminent historian and biblical scholar N. T. Wright has claimed that 'the crucifixion of Jesus is one of the best attested facts in ancient history'.[4] Liberal scholar J. D. Crossan, who rejects much of what is found in the Gospels, says, 'That he was crucified is as sure as anything historical can ever be.'[5] Even the renowned textual critic and agnostic professor Bart Ehrman, whose books criticizing Christianity have made him somewhat of a poster boy for sceptics, has said, 'One of the most certain facts of history is that Jesus was crucified on orders of the Roman prefect of Judea, Pontius Pilate.'[6] Why is the verdict from modern historians unanimous? It is simply because the historical evidence for the crucifixion is so strong.

Professor William Lane Craig, who has published voluminously on the history surrounding the life of Jesus, comments, 'Historians consider themselves to have hit historical pay dirt when they have *two* independent accounts of the same event.'[7] Yet for the crucifixion we have multiple attestations, from both Christian and non-Christian sources. Firstly, we have the four Gospels, Acts, the Pauline epistles, and the rest of the New Testament documents, which all date to the first century AD. It is undisputed that early Christianity from AD 33 had the crucifixion at the heart of its message. In addition to these sources we have the writings of the early Church Fathers, which are considered independent sources and date from the beginning of the second century. The Epistle of Ignatius (AD 110) to the Trallians says, 'He was truly persecuted under Pontius Pilate; He was truly crucified, and [truly] died, in the sight of beings in heaven, and on earth, and under the earth.'[8] He also attests to the crucifixion in his letters to the Smyrnaeans. Other early sources include the First Epistle of Clement to the church at Corinth, the letter of Polycarp to the Philippians, as well as numerous references in the works of Justin Martyr.

There is an equally impressive array of non-Christian sources, who would not have been biased towards the Christian interpretation, testifying to the historical fact of the crucifixion. The most important witnesses are from the historians Flavius Josephus and Cornelius Tacitus. Josephus was born around AD 37 to a priestly family in Jerusalem and would have known about the church from the very beginning. Eventually, Josephus ended up becoming a historian for the Roman Emperor Vespasian. There are two relevant places in his writings where Josephus mentions Jesus. In these passages, he mentions Jesus and His death by crucifixion under Pontius Pilate: 'And when Pilate, at the suggestion of the principal men amongst us, had condemned him to the cross . . .'[9]

Cornelius Tacitus was generally considered to be the best Roman historian and was known for accuracy and care in his work. In his last work, *Annals*, written in AD 116–117, he mentions the crucifixion of Jesus. Writing about a rumour that Nero was responsible for the fire of Rome he said, 'Consequently, to get rid of the report, Nero fastened the guilt and inflicted the most exquisite tortures on a class hated for their abominations, called Christians by the populace. Christus, from whom the name has its origin, suffered the extreme penalty during the reign of Tiberius at the hands of one of our procurators, Pontius Pilate.'[10] These two sources provide strong independent witness to the fact of the crucifixion. However, we also have some later references in the satirical writings of Lucian the Syrian. In his work *The Passing of Peregrinus* (AD 165), he mentions that Jesus was crucified in Palestine.[11] Then we also have a reference in the Babylonian Talmud, a source that would not have been friendly to the Christian position, which records that Jesus 'was hanged on the eve of the Passover' (*Sanhedrin* 43a). Being hanged on a tree was one way in which the Jewish people referred to crucifixion at that time.

In total, we have multiple attestations from both friendly and hostile witnesses that Jesus was crucified under Pontius Pilate in Jerusalem. In the words of Jewish scholar Geza Vermes, 'the passion is part of history'.[12] It was the passion of Jesus Christ that quite literally changed history.

Think about what we have looked at in this chapter. The Bible says that the cross is the greatest demonstration that God loves you. The crucifixion of Christ is one of the best-attested historical events, forever etched into the fabric of time. Therefore, we really can say that the fact that God loves us is one of the best-attested conclusions in the world. This means that the message of the cross is not just the message of some enlightened preacher, but the declaration of a real event, known by all, because Christianity is rooted in real history. The fact is this: you are loved by an eternal God; He proved it on the cross.

WHY SO FEW?

If this is true, why do so many people still reject the love of God? This is a difficult question, but perhaps the simplest way to find the answer is to ask another question: if you are not a Christian, or can remember a time before you were, why did you reject it? We make excuses! How can God get us to reciprocate His love? Some respond by saying that He could surely provide greater and more obvious evidence for His existence. However, God is not looking for people to simply believe in Him; He wants them to truly love Him. This does not require some undeniable proof of His existence—or else people would be compelled to believe in Him but still might not follow Him. God does not want our allegiance based merely on His power; He desires our love in response to His character.

How does the King win the love of His subjects? He lowers Himself to their level in order to make Himself known—and this is what we see in the incarnation of Jesus. This is the question that Søren Kierkegaard so beautifully addressed in his parable 'The King and the Maiden':

> Suppose there was a king who loved a humble maiden. The king was like no other king. Every statesman feared his wrath and dared not breathe a word of displeasure; every foreign state trembled before his power.
>
> And yet this mighty king was melted by love for a humble maiden who lived in a poor village in his kingdom. How could he declare his love for her? In an odd sort of way, his kingliness tied his hands. Thus, the king might have shown himself to the humble maiden in all the pomp of his power, causing the sun of his presence to rise over her cottage, shedding a glory over the scene, and making her forget herself in worshipful admiration. Alas, and

this might have satisfied the maiden, but it could not satisfy the king, who desired not his own glorification but hers.

If he brought her to the palace and crowned her head with jewels and clothed her body in royal robes, she would surely not resist—no one dared resist him. But would she love him? She would say she loved him, of course, but would she truly? Or would she live with him in fear, nursing a private grief for the life she had left behind? Would she be happy at his side?

If he rode to her forest cottage in his royal carriage, with an armed escort waving bright banners, that too would overwhelm her. He did not want a cringing subject. He wanted a lover, an equal. He wanted her to forget that he was a king and she a humble maiden and to let shared love cross the gulf between them. For it is only in love that the unequal can be made equal.

The king, convinced he could not elevate the maiden without crushing her freedom, resolved to descend to her. Clothed as a beggar, he approached her cottage with a worn cloak fluttering loose about him. This was not just a disguise—the king took on a totally new identity—He had renounced his throne to declare his love and to win hers.[13]

In this parable Kierkegaard beautifully expresses the same point that the apostle Paul teaches about Jesus, 'who, though he was in the form of God, did not count equality with God a thing to be grasped, but made himself nothing, taking the form of a servant, being born in the likeness of men. And being found in human form, he humbled himself by becoming obedient to the point of death, even death on a cross' (Philippians 2:6–8).

That God was willing to go to such great lengths to win your love should fill your heart with awe and wonder. Such contemplation has moved many to love the Saviour and lay down their lives in service of such a King—a King who would exchange a throne room for a manger and a crown for a cross; a King who would allow Himself to be forsaken, rejected and hated by those He longed to save; and ultimately a King who would lay down His life for those He loved. He truly deserves the title King of kings.

Oh the deep, deep love of Jesus!
Vast, unmeasured, boundless, free;
Rolling as a mighty ocean
In its fullness over me.
Underneath me, all around me,
Is the current of thy love;
Leading onward, leading homeward,
To thy glorious rest above.
(Samuel Trevor Francis, 1875)

NOTES OVERLEAF ➡

Notes

1 'Romeo and Juliet Translation', Act 2, Scene 2, SparkNotes, 2005, https://www.sparknotes.com/nofear/shakespeare/romeojuliet/page_80/.

2 Ibid., Act 5, Scene 3, https://www.sparknotes.com/nofear/shakespeare/romeojuliet/page_286/.

3 C. S. Lewis, *God in the Dock* (Grand Rapids: Eerdmans, 1970), p. 49.

4 'NT Wright: Why Jesus' Crucifixion Is a Fact of History', Premier Christianity blog, 13 April 2017, https://www.premierchristianity.com/Blog/NT-Wright-Why-Jesus-crucifixion-is-a-fact-of-history.

5 J. D. Crossan, *Jesus: A Revolutionary Biography* (New York: Harper Collins, 1994), p. 145.

6 Bart Erhman, *The Historical Jesus: Lecture Transcript and Course Guidebook* ([n.p.]: The Teaching Company, 2000), p. 162.

7 William Lane Craig, 'Question of the Week: #103 Independent Sources for Jesus' Burial and Empty Tomb', *Reasonable Faith*, 6 April 2009, https://www.reasonablefaith.org/question-answer/P20/independent-sources-for-jesus-burial-and-empty-tomb.

8 Ignatius of Antioch, *The Epistle of Ignatius to the Trallians*, Early Christian Writings, http://www.earlychristianwritings.com/text/ignatius-trallians-longer.html.

9 Josephus, *Antiquities of the Jews* 18.63, Perseus Digital Library, http://www.perseus.tufts.edu/hopper/text?doc=Perseus%3Atext%3A1999.01.0146%3Abook%3D18%3Asection%3D63.

10 Tacitus, *The Annals of Tacitus* 15.44, Early Christian Writings, http://www.earlychristianwritings.com/text/annals.html.

11 Lucian of Samosata, *The Passing of Peregrinus* 11.

12 Geza Vermes, *The Passion: The True Story of an Event That Changed Human History* (New York: Penguin, 2006), p. 9.

13 Søren Kierkegaard, *Philosophical Fragments* ([n.p.]: Rough Draft Printing, 2013), pp. 26–34.

8 I am adopted

IT WAS THE WORST OF TIMES

'It was the best of times, it was the worst of times' is how Charles Dickens famously described the situation in London in his book *A Tale of Two Cities* (1859). His novels provide us with many fascinating descriptions of nineteenth-century London. Dickens spent most of his life in old London, walking the streets and taking in the sights and smells. His descriptive mastery and literary genius allow modern readers to immerse themselves in a bygone age. Queen Victoria ascended to the throne in 1837, a time when the 'sun never set' on the British Empire. Vast wealth poured into the empire, fuelling the Industrial Revolution and urbanization of the cities. By 1880 the number of people living in London had swelled to over four million.

Unfortunately, this huge surge of productivity and wealth did nothing to alleviate the desperate poverty of the working classes. The overcrowding in the inner cities led to the formation of slums, known as 'rookeries' because they held so many people. Lodging was cramped, with up to twenty people sharing a single room without sanitation or running water. These slums had little or no lighting; they were filthy, squalid places. They were notorious for housing all manner of criminal deviants who made up London's seedy underbelly. Robbery, pickpocketing, prostitution and violence were daily occurrences. London had a cheap gin shop on every street corner, which added to the vice and misery. The black smog from a thousand chimney pots filled the air, leaving a layer of soot over everything like fresh morning dew. With no sewers serving the city, raw sewage and unimaginable filth flowed through the streets into the river Thames, often mixing with the city's drinking water. At one point, the Thames became such a cesspit of sewage and waste that the stench could be smelt throughout the whole city! This episode, dubbed 'the Great Stink' of 1854, resulted in a parliamentary call for action. These deplorable conditions meant that disease was rife; cholera (from contaminated water), dysentery and tuberculosis claimed many lives.

This was Dickens' London. His writings give us an insight into the realities of Victorian living. Although the rain was needed to wash away the filth from the streets, rain in London was not a refreshing thing. Dickens, in *Little Dorrit*, describes it this way: 'In the country, the rain would have developed a thousand fresh scents, and every drop would have had its bright association with some beautiful form of growth or life. In the city, it developed only foul stale smells, and was a sickly, lukewarm, dirt-stained, wretched addition to the gutters.'[1]

Elsewhere, Dickens talks about the live cattle markets and slaughterhouses that were held in the middle of the city, adding an unknown amount of animal excrement and blood to the already foul mix of human sewage:

> In half a quarter of a mile's length of Whitechapel, at one time, there shall be six hundred newly slaughtered oxen hanging up, and seven hundred sheep—but, the more the merrier—proof of prosperity. Hard by Snow Hill and Warwick Lane, you shall see

the little children, inured to sights of brutality from their birth, trotting along the alleys, mingled with troops of horribly busy pigs, up to their ankles in blood—but it makes the young rascals hardy. Into the imperfect sewers of this overgrown city, you shall have the immense mass of corruption, engendered by these practices, lazily thrown out of sight, to rise, in poisonous gases, into your house at night, when your sleeping children will most readily absorb them, and to find its languid way, at last, into the river that you drink.[2]

In the novel *Oliver Twist*, Dickens describes the scene as Oliver travels through the infamous Smithfield live cattle market in London:

Countrymen, butchers, drovers, hawkers, boys, thieves, idlers, and vagabonds of every low grade, were mingled together in a mass; the whistling of drovers, the barking dogs, the bellowing and plunging of the oxen, the bleating of sheep, the grunting and squeaking of pigs, the cries of hawkers, the shouts, oaths, and quarrelling on all sides; the ringing of bells and roar of voices, that issued from every public-house; the crowding, pushing, driving, beating, whooping and yelling; the hideous and discordant din that resounded from every corner of the market; and the unwashed, unshaven, squalid, and dirty figures constantly running to and fro, and bursting in and out of the throng; rendered it a stunning and bewildering scene, which quite confounded the senses.[3]

Due to the circumstances of his young life, in which his father had fallen into financial difficulty and was imprisoned in Marshalsea debtors' prison, along with Charles's mother and younger siblings, Charles himself was sent to work alone at a boot-blacking factory. Dickens became a voice for the poor and destitute, often highlighting their plight through his writings. Of particular disgust to Dickens was the new Poor Law of 1834. This law stopped all funding of local parish poorhouses and established the workhouse system. Workhouses became little more than prisons; they were a cruel provision, aimed at deterring people from seeking poor relief, and only the most vulnerable and desperate would go to them. A life of forced labour for minimal food and shelter awaited on the inside. The workhouses were run by local guardians who were often vicious and harsh. *Oliver Twist* is famous for highlighting the conditions of the workhouse system. The orphan Oliver suffers all manner of punishment in the workhouse. Starved, beaten, threatened and publicly flogged, he eventually escapes and ends up on the streets of London working for a gang of child pickpockets under the command of the villainous Fagin.

THINK OF THE CHILDREN

Inevitably, the people to suffer most in such an environment were the vulnerable of society: the sick, the elderly and, tragically, the children. Infant mortality was so high in London that one-third of all children would die before reaching five years of age. Children had no rights, and many were orphaned and destitute. Many children were forced to work fourteen-hour days in the factories or mines. Boys as young as four would often become 'climbing boys', owned by chimney sweeps and forced to climb up the chimneys of the wealthy. This was a dangerous occupation, with a high mortality rate through suffocation and contraction of respiratory diseases.

The plight of these orphans and destitute children was taken up by primarily Nonconformist evangelical Christians whose faith and belief in the inherent dignity of all people motivated them to practical acts of charity. The congregational minister Andrew Reed, known as 'the orphans' friend', worked tirelessly for the rights and dignity of the outcasts of society. He founded the London Orphan Society in 1840, the Infant Orphan Asylum (now the Royal National Children's Foundation) and the Reedham Orphanage. He was a pioneer of his time, seeking to provide a dignified life for those with learning disabilities.

Lord Shaftesbury (the 7th Earl of Shaftesbury) was also a tireless defender of the poor who campaigned in Parliament for their rights, seeking to reduce working hours for factory children and to improve the conditions for a host of others. In a parliamentary speech, Lord Shaftesbury claimed that there were '30,000 naked, filthy, roaming, lawless, and deserted children' living on the streets of London.[4] Most would not live into their teens. So disgusted was he with the treatment of these children that he compared what he witnessed in his day to those who in ancient times sacrificed children to the god Moloch. He even claimed that the latter

> were a merciful people compared with Englishmen in the nineteenth century. For those nations destroyed at once their wretched offspring, and prevented a long career of suffering and crime; but we, having sucked out every energy of body and of soul, tossed them on the world a mass of skin and bone, incapable of exertion, brutalised in their understanding, and disqualified for immortality.[5]

The Earl's efforts received warm approval from many in society. The English poet and historian Robert Southey wrote to Shaftesbury:

Thousands of thousands will bless you for taking up the cause of these poor children. I do not believe that anything more inhuman than the system has ever disgraced human nature, in any age or country. Was I not right in saying that Moloch is a more merciful friend than Mammon? Death in the brazen arms of the Carthaginian idol was mercy to the slow waste of life in the factories. God bless you![6]

Shaftesbury was motivated by his Christian faith, evidenced by his involvement with the Church Missionary Society, the British and Foreign Bible Society and the Religious Tract Society. He described himself as an 'Evangelical of Evangelicals'. He died in the year 1885. His funeral was held in Westminster Abbey, and thousands of people crowded into Parliament Square to catch a glimpse of his funeral procession. In addition to the usual dignitaries, the mass of people included throngs of the working classes he had served so diligently: mill-workers, bootblack boys, factory hands, ragged school children and similar. Representatives from hundreds of charitable institutions were also present at the memorial service in the Abbey. An important biography of Shaftesbury claims, 'No man has in fact ever done more to lessen the extent of human misery or to add to the sum total of human happiness.'[7] Shaftesbury was a friend of the preacher C. H. Spurgeon, even residing over the celebrations for the latter's fiftieth birthday. Three days after Shaftesbury's death, Spurgeon preached a sermon in which he said this about him:

During the past week the church of God, and the world at large, have sustained a very serious loss. In the taking home to himself by our gracious Lord of the Earl of Shaftesbury, we have, in my judgment, lost the best man of the age . . . He was a man most

> true in his personal piety, as I know from having enjoyed his private friendship; a man most firm in his faith in the gospel of our Lord Jesus Christ; a man intensely active in the cause of God and truth . . . We shall not know for many a year how much we miss in missing him; how great an anchor he was for this drifting generation, and how great a stimulus he was to every movement for the benefit of the poor. Both man and beast may unite in mourning him: he was the friend of every living thing. He lived for the oppressed; he lived for London; he lived for the nation; he lived still more for God. He has finished his course; and though we do not lay him to sleep in the grave with the sorrow of those who have no hope, yet we cannot but mourn that a great man and a prince has fallen this day in Israel.[8]

Perhaps it was the example of Lord Shaftesbury that inspired Spurgeon to partner with Thomas Barnardo years later and start their orphanages. Barnardo's is still the largest children's charity in the UK today. Whatever the case, these Christian reformers were motivated by a sense of calling regarding the children, orphans, destitute and helpless. But the question we must ask is 'Why?'

ADOPTION INTO THE FAMILY OF GOD

One of the most cherished and comforting truths in the Christian faith is that of adoption. This is the teaching that, when a person becomes a Christian, they are adopted into an intimate, loving family. 'Father' is an utterly unique designation for God; it is warm and familial, indicating the type of relationship that a Christian has with God. God's heart is always for the fatherless. The Bible declares that God is 'Father of the fatherless and protector of widows' (Psalm 68:5) and that Christians should 'Give justice to the weak and the fatherless; maintain the right of the afflicted and the destitute' (Psalm 82:3). God's description of true religion is 'to look after orphans and widows in their distress' (James 1:27 NIV). This is God's heart because He is not merely like a father in some metaphorical way, but He actually *is* a father, a perfect heavenly Father, who gives us a true and impeccable understanding of what true fatherhood should encompass.

Many in this world understand the longing for the love of a father, yet have never experienced it. We do not have to look far to see the effects a bad father can have on his children, or to see the tragic results of a generation growing up without fathers in their lives. The truth of adoption contained within the gospel is the cure for this malady. The mission of Jesus is to invite people to know the heavenly Father, but it is more than that: it is an invitation to be adopted into the family of God, so that we can relate to the Almighty in a personal and intimate way as His children. God says, 'I will make my dwelling among them and walk among them, and I will be their God, and they shall be my people . . . I will be a father to you, and you shall be sons and daughters to me' (2 Corinthians 6:16, 18). Elsewhere, the apostle John writes, 'See what kind of love the Father has given to us, that we should be called children of God; and so we are' (1 John 3:1).

Understanding this principle of adoption and of relating to God as our Father is essential to correctly grasping the uniqueness of Christianity. Only in the Trinitarian concept of God do we have the capacity to experience the love of the heavenly Father and to be adopted into a loving family. As J. I. Packer put it so beautifully in his classic book *Knowing God*,

You sum up the whole of New Testament religion if you describe it as the knowledge of God as one's holy Father. If you want to judge how well a person understands Christianity, find out how much he makes of the thought of being God's child, and having God as his Father. If this is not the thought that prompts and controls his worship and prayers and his whole outlook on life, it means that he does not understand Christianity very well at all.[9]

JESUS AS THE WAY

The concept of God as Father is integral to the gospel. In John 14:6 Jesus uttered these famous words: 'I am the way, and the truth, and the life. No one comes to the Father except through me.' Usually when this verse is quoted, it is used to explain that Jesus is the only way of salvation. That is obviously true, and salvation is implicit in the statement, but the way Jesus chooses to describe Himself is not as the 'way to salvation' but as the way 'to the Father'. The mission of Jesus, which is global in its scope and unparalleled in its impact, is to introduce people to a relationship with the Father by becoming His sons and daughters. This focus takes the subject of salvation away from dry and mechanical formulas and places it in the context of an intimate family living room.

Jesus was on earth to display the Father's love for mankind, so all His words and deeds must be understood in this light. Only Christ, God's Son, was fit for such a task. Jesus is said to be the 'radiance of the glory of God and the exact imprint of [God's] nature' (Hebrews 1:3). As such, Jesus could rightly proclaim that He is one with the Father (John 10:30) and that 'Whoever has seen me has seen the Father' (John 14:9). Christ came to show mankind that the Father loves them just as much as He loves Jesus His Son (John 17:23). Think about this for a moment; it is the glorious truth of adoption.

The purpose of the cross was to clear the way, the barrier that sin had created—but the way to what? The way into the Father's presence—the most glorious destination possible: one that transcends anything mortal man could conceive, that represents all the power and justice, all the holiness and goodness, all the mercy and grace that is abundant in the richness of God's character. Yet it is also the place where the Father's love is most wondrously and gloriously manifest in its purest form as the dwelling place of the Godhead. This destination—this journey—is into the very heart of the Father. This is the message of the gospel. We do not come to the Father as strangers, as orphans, as those who are unworthy, but by the finished work of Christ we come to Him as sons and daughters. Simply amazing!

THE SPIRIT'S ROLE IN ADOPTION

In adoption we are placed into the family of God. The Bible says that 'in love [God] predestined us for adoption as sons through Jesus Christ' (Ephesians 1:5). It is the role of the Holy Spirit to witness to this truth, and that is why He is given to us as a guarantee of our sonship. In the fullness of time Jesus came so that 'we might receive adoption as sons. And because you are sons, God has sent the Spirit of his Son into our hearts, crying, "Abba! Father!"' (Galatians 4:5–6). Elsewhere, the apostle Paul puts it even more clearly: 'For you did not receive the spirit of slavery to fall back into fear, but you have received the Spirit of adoption as sons, by whom we cry, "Abba! Father!" The Spirit himself bears witness with our spirit that we are children of God' (Romans 8:15–16).

It is this Spirit of adoption, living in us if we are Christians, that makes us cry out, 'Father!' It is the union we have with Christ by the Spirit's work that provides the means for us to have such an undeserved level of intimacy with the holy God. This is a great blessing of salvation. Not only are we redeemed from being in slavery to sin, but we are set free and placed into a family, the family of the one true God. When we cry out for something, we are expressing a deep emotional longing for that thing. It is usually something that our whole being is searching for; in the case of the Christian, that longing is for the Father. Unlike the endless longings for the things of the world that go unfulfilled, the longing for the Father's heart is fulfilled in the Christian's life by the work of the Son and the gift of the Spirit. We are recipients of a grace that is truly unsearchable!

It was this teaching of adoption that those great Victorian reformers understood from personal experience and which motivated them to share the Father's heart. They cried out in the world for the orphan and the destitute because, being ambassadors of Christ, they were representing the values of a heavenly kingdom on this earth.

IF SONS, THEN HEIRS ALSO?

If this were all it meant, it would be more than we could ever comprehend, but the Scriptures testify to even greater blessing resulting from our being adopted. In both the Galatians and Romans texts we are told that we are not only sons but also heirs with Christ:

So you are no longer a slave, but a son, and if a son, then an heir through God.

(Galatians 4:7)

The Spirit himself bears witness with our spirit that we are children of God, and if children, then heirs—heirs of God and fellow heirs with Christ, provided we suffer with him in order that we may also be glorified with him.

(Romans 8:16–17)

Theologians are generally united in their understanding that Paul is drawing upon the Roman practice of adoption of his time. In Roman adoption, not only was an adopted son given a new name and a new family, but he also received the right to an inheritance. As a Christian, you are an heir of God and a fellow heir with Christ. You have an 'inheritance that is imperishable, undefiled, and unfading, kept in heaven for you' (1 Peter 1:4). Through adoption the Father 'has qualified you to share in the inheritance of the saints in light' (Colossians 1:12). This inheritance includes many things that cannot fully be described: the Bible describes them as 'the unsearchable riches of Christ' (Ephesians 3:8). As a co-heir of Christ, you are privileged to share in everything that the Father will give to the Son. But what is this?

Surely it will take eternity to reveal everything that God has prepared for those who love him. Hebrews 1:1–2 says that 'God spoke to our fathers by the prophets, but in these last days he has spoken to us by his Son, whom he appointed the heir of all things'. The phrase 'heir of all things' means just that: everything! Absolutely everything is included in this inheritance. It is the greatest inheritance that anyone could ever receive. It includes all the facets of our salvation:

the redemption, the forgiveness, the mercy and the grace. But it also includes our adoption by none other than the Father Himself! We are His, and He is ours. It also includes that future glorification of our bodies, our eternal life and existence in the heavenly kingdom with Him.

Quite literally, by a sheer act of God's undeserved favour, we are given everything that belongs to Christ. Such a statement at first glance seems extremely presumptuous, yet it is what the Scriptures teach. But this is no cheap grace, no trivial thing. God does not promise us all these things right now; on this the Bible is quite clear. Paul says that we will share this inheritance 'provided we suffer with [Christ] in order that we may also be glorified with him' (Romans 8:16–17)—yet he also assures us that 'the sufferings of this present time are not worth comparing with the glory that is to be revealed to us' (8:18). Simply put, because of Jesus we have everything.

The following anecdote helps us to grasp some of these precious truths:

Years ago, there was a wealthy man who, along with his son, travelled the world collecting great works of art. They owned many priceless treasures—paintings by Picasso and Rembrandt and many others. The father had lost his wife many years ago, and he did everything with his son; his son was his entire world.

Then war broke out in their nation and the son was conscripted into the army. Tragically, the son was killed in battle whilst trying to rescue a friend.

Shortly after receiving the news about his son, the father was visited by a young man. At the porch of his house, the young man said to him, 'Sir, my name is Richard. You don't know me, but your son saved my life. He was shot while carrying me to safety after a grenade landed near me during an ambush. I saw him save many people that day.'

The father, eyes filled with tears, thanked the young man for telling him.

But the young man continued, 'He would often talk about you at night when the guns were silent. He told stories of your journeys collecting art from around the world.' He then took out a package from his bag and handed it to the father. 'I love to paint too, and I painted this of your son one night. I'm not particularly good, but I think he would want you to have it.'

The father loved the painting, and he had it hung proudly above his office desk.

Years later when the father passed away, his estate, including his great works of art, was auctioned off. Dignitaries and collectors came from far and wide for the opportunity to purchase his collection. The auctioneer brought out the first painting to be auctioned. It was the portrait of the son. The crowd became agitated, unimpressed by this unknown piece of art.

The auctioneer began, 'Who will start the bidding at £1,000? £500? £100?'

There were groans of disgust from the restless audience.

The auctioneer again said, 'Who will give me £50 for the son? Will anyone take the son?'

Eventually, a man at the back shouted, 'I'll give you £20 for it.' The man was a scruffy-looking gentleman who was clearly out of place among the wealthy audience. However, he was the groundsman of the estate and he remembered the son fondly, but he couldn't afford to make a higher offer.

'Sold for £20,' declared the auctioneer, as he banged the gavel.

An eager member of the crowd shouted, 'Now bring out the real stuff.' But the auctioneer walked to the centre of the stage and said to the audience, 'I'm sorry, but the auction is now over.'

The angry audience began to boo loudly. The auctioneer continued, 'There was a secret stipulation in the will that when the auction began, the first painting to be sold must be this portrait.

Whoever decided to buy this painting would then inherit the entire estate. So the man who chose the son gets everything.'[10]

NOTES OVERLEAF ➡

Notes

1 Charles Dickens, *Little Dorrit*, Book 1, Chapter 3 (1855–1857), http://www.victorianlondon.org/books/dorrit-03.htm.

2 From 'A Moment of French Folly', article for *Households Words,* March 1851, quoted at 'Dickens' London', The Charles Dickens Page, http://charlesdickenspage.com/dickens_london.html.

3 Charles Dickens, *Oliver Twist*, Penguin Classics (London: Penguin, 2003), p. 171.

4 Hugh Cunningham, *The Invention of Childhood* (London: BBC Books, 2006), p. 162.

5 Edwin Hodder, *The Life and Work of the Seventh Earl of Shaftesbury, K. G.*, Vol. 1 (London: Cassel & Co., 1892; repr. Cambridge: Cambridge University Press, 2014), p. 155.

6 Ibid., p. 157.

7 Georgina Battiscombe, *Shaftesbury: A Biography of the Seventh Earl, 1801–1885* (London: Constable, 1974), p. 334.

8 'Departed Saints Yet Living', *The Metropolitan Tabernacle Pulpit Sermons*, Vol. 31 (London: Passmore & Alabaster, 1885), pp. 541–542.

9 J. I. Packer, *Knowing God* (Downers Grove, IL: InterVarsity Press, 1973), p. 182.

10 Story available widely on the Internet but rewritten here in my own words; original source unknown.

9 I am called

The longing of the human heart for some sort of higher purpose often compels us to search for it in all the wrong places. We can, for example, spend our entire lives trying to reach the top of our profession, to help as many people as possible or to earn as much money as we can, and only when this imaginary line is crossed will we consider ourselves successful. Only then can we conclude that we have found our purpose in life. However, a story emerged in the British press recently about the UK's youngest lottery winner. She was preparing to sue the lottery bosses for ruining her life. In an interview she said, 'People look at me and think, "I wish I had her lifestyle, I wish I had her money." But they don't realise the extent of my stress. I have material things but apart from that my life is empty. What is my purpose in life?'[1]

Material things do not lead to fulfilment in life. There is an inner cry for purpose that transcends the physical things of this world. For the Christian, this desire finds its satisfaction in understanding that, because we are created in the image of God and are now part of the body of Christ, every one of us is called to be part of something bigger than ourselves. We are citizens of the kingdom of God and we all have a part to play in this kingdom. Understanding our calling as Christians is the key to living a fulfilled life. Os Guinness defines 'calling' in the following way: 'calling is the truth that God calls us to himself so decisively that everything we are, everything we do, and everything we have is invested with a special devotion and dynamism lived out as a response to his summons and service.'[2]

The calling we have as Christians is like no other calling in the world. It comes from the highest possible authority. It is a call to be involved in the work of God. It is a holy calling. Nothing in this world can compare with it. True, there are many noble and wonderful works that people accomplish, but the Christian's calling is one that looks towards and builds into an eternal kingdom. Such a calling means that your life can never be considered empty or meaningless, no matter what activity you are engaged in. God's calling infuses every moment of your life with significance and meaning. He will use your past, present and future as He draws you closer to Himself. With God, even the ordinary becomes extraordinary because it is part of something bigger. His plan and purpose for your life is part of His eternal plan for the destiny of mankind.

As we have discovered with the subject of identity and meaning, the question of calling and purpose is only satisfactorily answered by keeping God firmly in the equation. The moment we evict God, we remove the only sure foundation we have for our lives. If we reject God, our calling goes unanswered. We are forced to rely on ourselves to try to pull together some purpose from this world. This will usually be connected to our own achievements. At best, this will only ever be a temporary calling, a confidence in ourselves, in riches, position or power, none of which can provide mankind with a transcendent purpose. Why? Simply because if mankind is truly made for God, then only God can give a calling specifically tailored for each individual.

This is exactly what God has done for every Christian. The true secret to finding your calling is to realize that it comes from God and that a fundamental aspect of the Christian life is allowing God to have authority over you; to put it another way, this means laying yourself aside. This was the spirit behind the words of John the Baptist, whose calling was to prepare the way for Jesus. When his disciples came and told him that Jesus was also baptizing and that people were going to Him, rather than seeing Jesus as someone in competition with him for the crowd's attention John recognized that he had fulfilled his calling and he said, 'Therefore this joy of mine is now complete. He must increase, but I must decrease' (John 3:29–30). In his conclusion in *Mere Christianity*, C. S. Lewis echoes this thought and gives us the answer to finding who we truly are and what we are here for:

> The more we get what we now call 'ourselves' out of the way and let Him take us over, the more truly ourselves we become. There is so much of Him that millions and millions of 'little Christs', all different, will still be too few to express Him fully. He made them all. He invented—as an author invents characters in a novel—all the different men that you and I were intended to be. In that sense our real selves are all waiting for us in Him. It is no good trying to 'be myself' without Him. The more I resist Him and try to live on my own, the more I become dominated by my own heredity and upbringing and surroundings and natural desires. In fact, what I so proudly call 'Myself' becomes merely the meeting place for trains of events which I never started and which I cannot stop.[3]

Ultimately because it is only God who truly knows us, finding who we are and what our calling is can only come from knowing Him.

YOU ARE AN AMBASSADOR

It is the great privilege of every Christian to be enlisted in the service of God. The particular way God uses people will vary greatly from person to person. Yet every single one of us who has been redeemed by Christ is given the title of ambassador. An ambassador is a special diplomat sent by another state to be its representative in a foreign country. As long as ambassadors are on foreign soil, they are there as representatives of their home nation and everything they do will reflect upon that nation. To be an ambassador is a high calling and responsibility.

In God's eyes, we are his ambassadors. The apostle Paul made this announcement to the Christians living in the Greek city of Corinth:

> Therefore, if anyone is in Christ, he is a new creation. The old has passed away; behold, the new has come. All this is from God, who through Christ reconciled us to himself and gave us the ministry of reconciliation; that is, in Christ God was reconciling the world to himself, not counting their trespasses against them, and entrusting to us the message of reconciliation. Therefore, we are ambassadors for Christ, God making his appeal through us. We implore you on behalf of Christ, be reconciled to God. For our sake he made him to be sin who knew no sin, so that in him we might become the righteousness of God. (2 Corinthians 5:17–21)

We are Christ's ambassadors. This description fits the Christian life perfectly. We have become members of God's kingdom; as the apostle Paul says, 'our citizenship is in heaven' (Philippians 3:20). We have an eternal identity and citizenship in God's kingdom. Paul also says, 'So then you are no longer strangers and aliens, but you are fellow citizens with the saints and members of the household of God' (Ephesians 2:19). As such, we will always feel slightly out of place in this world—or at least we should, if we are properly concerned with the values of our Father's house—for we know that we are

strangers and exiles on the earth. For people who speak thus make it clear that they are seeking a homeland. If they had been thinking of that land from which they had gone out, they would have had opportunity to return. But as it is, they desire a better country, that is, a heavenly one. Therefore God is not ashamed to be called their God, for he has prepared for them a city. (Hebrews 11:13–16)

It is said that home is where your heart is, so if our hearts are with Christ, there will always be part of us that can only find satisfaction in Him. C. S. Lewis captured this feeling brilliantly:

If I find in myself a desire which no experience in this world can satisfy, the most probable explanation is that I was made for another world . . . I must keep alive in myself the desire for my true country, which I shall not find till after death; I must never let it get snowed under or turned aside; I must make it the main object of life to press on to that country and to help others to do the same.[4]

We desire that 'better country' and we know that, because of the work of Christ, our ultimate destiny is that we belong there. It is our homeland. Lewis depicts this in his world of Narnia using Aslan's country figuratively of heaven. In *The Last Battle*, Jewel the unicorn describes their homecoming: 'I have come home at last! This is my real country! I belong here. This is the land I have been looking for all my life, though I never knew it till now. The reason why we loved the old Narnia is that it sometimes looked a little like this . . . Come further up, come further in!'[5]

FOR SUCH A TIME AS THIS

As ambassadors of Christ, Christians belong to a different kingdom from the one to which most people they share this earth with belong. Yet they do not just look passively to the future; they are called to be God's representatives here and now. Christians have been placed exactly where they are for such a time as this, precisely because God wants them to be here. God is building His kingdom now, and He is using His people to do this. Christians are to stand for Christ, His values and His kingdom, all the while living as strangers and pilgrims in this world. The ambassador's job is to represent Him now: to speak in His name, to seek to love what He loves and to hate what He hates; to show love, mercy and compassion in His name; to be concerned with justice and righteousness in His name; and to look to fulfil that ministry of reconciliation whereby people can be saved and enter the fullness of life that Jesus has promised. A Christian is commissioned by Jesus Himself to be His witness (Acts 1:8). We are on a rescue mission, and it is a lifetime responsibility and privilege to be a part of God's kingdom.

If you are a Christian, you are an ambassador. As God's ambassador your entire life is a mission trip, and no one person is greater than another. There is only One who is great, and He is your King, the one from whom you receive the strength to fulfil your role here on earth. Everything you do and everywhere you go, you do it as an ambassador for Christ. The next time you feel unworthy, the next time you fail, or wonder how you can be doing God's work during the regular nine-to-five routine of life, remember that you are called for such a time as this—that God has work for you to do right where you are. You were created for a purpose. The Bible says you 'are his workmanship, created in Christ Jesus for good works, which God prepared beforehand, that [you] should walk in them' (Ephesians 2:10). Think about that: you are His work, His masterpiece; and in the counsel of His own will, God has already prepared good works for you to do, and these works will echo into eternity.

In light of this, we must ask ourselves several questions. Are we willing to live lives worthy of the calling we have as Christ's ambassadors? Are we willing to lay ourselves aside in order that Christ may have the number one position in our lives? In short, are we ready for the mission? Will we answer the call?

Our lives here on this earth are really just a vapour (James 4:14). We can take nothing that we gain, earn or achieve to heaven with us; only the treasures that we store in heaven will last.

I conclude with a few verses of a poem from the British cricketer C. T. Studd, who became a missionary to China:

Give me Father, a purpose deep,
In joy or sorrow Thy word to keep;
Faithful and true whatever the strife,
Pleasing Thee in my daily life;
Only one life, 'twill soon be past,
Only what's done for Christ will last.

Oh let my love with fervour burn,
And from the world now let me turn;

Living for Thee, and Thee alone,
Bringing Thee pleasure on Thy throne;
Only one life, 'twill soon be past,
Only what's done for Christ will last.

Only one life, yes only one,
Now let me say, 'Thy will be done';
And when at last I'll hear the call,
I know I'll say ''twas worth it all';
Only one life, 'twill soon be past,
Only what's done for Christ will last.

WHO AM I?

Notes

1 Maya Oppenheim, 'Britain's Youngest Euromillions Winner Drops Plans to Sue Lottery Bosses for "Ruining Her Life"', Independent.co.uk, 16 February 2017, http://www.independent.co.uk/news/uk/home-news/jane-park-euromillions-winner-youngest-drops-sue-lottery-bosses-ruined-life-loose-women-a7583326.html.

2 Os Guinness, *The Call: Finding and Fulfilling the Central Purpose of Your Life* (Nashville: Word, 1998), p. 4.

3 C. S. Lewis, *Mere Christianity* (London: Harper Collins, 2002), p. 225.

4 Ibid., p. 137.

5 C. S. Lewis, *The Last Battle*, The Chronicles of Narnia (London: Harper Collins, 2009), p. 210.

10 Afterword

So now is the time: the hour has come. We have surveyed the question of what it means to be human and seen that the truth lies in understanding not only where we came from, but also what we were made for. From these questions spring all the issues of life.

When I first delivered a lecture based on some of the material in this book, a man ran up to me afterwards, a little agitated, and blurted out, 'You never answered the questions "What does it mean to be human and what is the purpose of life?"' I was a little taken aback, thinking that surely I had implicitly answered both of these with all the material I had covered in the previous hour. However, I later realized that what this man was really looking for was a concise summation of all the data that he could take away to learn and apply for himself, a sort of modern-day creed. The word 'creed' comes from the Latin word *credo*, 'I believe', and creeds operate as a formal summary of what a group believes. Since giving that first talk I now include at the end what I have called 'The Anthropic Creed', which briefly summarizes the Christian viewpoint of human identity. The Anthropic Creed is as follows:

> That mankind is a uniquely designed creation, distinct from the animal kingdom, fashioned with the privilege of being an image-bearer of the Almighty God. We were designed to live in a relationship with Him, but the entrance of sin severed this relationship. Only through the redemption offered by His Son can

we reclaim this sacred purpose, whereby we are free to love, glorify and enjoy Him for ever. We are called as ambassadors to fulfil the works that He has prepared for us on this earth, as He prepares us for an eternity with Him!

HOW WILL YOU ANSWER THE CALL?

The questions of who we are and what the purpose of our lives is both hinge upon how we respond to two statements that Jesus made to his followers two thousand years ago. The first is this: 'Who do you say that I am?' (Matthew 16:15). If we respond that Jesus is the Christ, the Son of the living God, as Peter did, then we must also accept that His record of humanity is final—we now know what we are! The second is His challenge to those who answered the first question correctly: His summons 'Follow me' (Matthew 4:19). It is such a seemingly simple statement, yet within it lie all the mysteries of life. This is our call, our purpose, and what sets us apart as those who can rightly say we have found the meaning of life.

All their life in this world and all their adventures in Narnia had only been the cover and the title page: now at last they were beginning Chapter One of the Great Story, which no one on earth has read; which goes on forever; in which every chapter is better than the one before.[1]

Soli Deo Gloria.

His master said to him, 'Well done, good and faithful servant. You have been faithful over a little; I will set you over much. Enter into the joy of your master.' (Matthew 25:21)

Note

1 C. S. Lewis, *The Last Battle*, The Chronicles of Narnia (London: Harper Collins, 2009), p. 224.

WHO AM I?